Dreaming Your World Into Being

The Shaman's Secrets to Having the Life You Desire Now

Jon Rasmussen

Published by Jon Rasmussen

DEAR NELLIE,
THANK YOU FOR YOUR
TREMENDOUS SUPPORT AND
POWERFUL PRESENCE AND IMPACT
IN THE WORLD. MUCH LOVE,
Jon Rasm—
3/3/09

Dreaming Your World Into Being: The Shaman's Secrets to Having the Life You Desire Now

Copyright© 2008 by Jon Rasmussen

Published and distributed in the United States of America by: Jon Rasmussen.

Library of Congress Control Number: 2008904120

ISBN: 978-0-615-20302-7

Contents

Dreaming Your World Into Being

❧

Prologue

By reading this book, you are playing an active and deliberate role in creating the life you desire and a world of greater beauty, joy, peace, pleasure, exhilaration, health, well-being, and abundance for generations to come. You are dreaming a new reality into being while you are wide-awake. You will be creating not only new experiences for yourself, but the influence of your new dream will reverberate through all of Creation, and have a measurable impact on our collective experience of the World that can last for decades and beyond. Everyone on the planet is already influencing the World dream, whether deliberately or not, but the deliberate dreaming is the most influential because of the underlying clarity and power of intention behind it. This book is meant to guide all of us into a more conscious and deliberate vision, so that together we are more powerfully, freely, and joyfully "dreaming the world into being."

Some of you may already be asking the question, "What does he mean by *dreaming* a new reality into being?" "How can such a passive activity make anything happen?" When I first heard of this concept, I asked the same questions. As a budding young scientist, I needed clear answers and plenty of proof; otherwise, it was all just too fanciful for me. After twenty-plus years of intense study and experience, I think that I may have come across a few solid answers. I also discovered that there were more secrets to the process and ultimate success of dreaming into being than have been presented in popular works such as "What the Bleep Do We Know," "The Secret," and "Ask and It is Given." And these secrets are revealed in the simple techniques and worldview that I learned from the Shamans.

Some of my advisors have suggested that I really have written two or three books here: A treatise on my experiences and views of Shamanism, a partial autobiography, and the secrets and vision for dreaming the world into being. I thought seriously about taking their advice to divide this into two or three separate books, but I felt it was important to follow the sequence that I have presented here. Through sharing with you what I have learned and experienced, I hope to have provided a sufficiently detailed foundation in the first parts of this book, such that it may make sense enough to you in your own life experiences, in order to move forward with the process of dreaming your world into being. It takes us on a longer journey towards the vision, but hopefully a journey full of richness and rewards that are worthy of your time. And of course, you will know what feels best for you, and skip around accordingly.

My simplest way of explaining this concept and action of dreaming while awake, is that it is similar to the act of daydreaming that we are all familiar with; but, it takes it much farther. Do you remember any of the fanciful daydreams you've had throughout your life, usually sitting in school or at work? And remember how your teacher or boss promptly snapped you out of them? Perhaps the more accepted way of daydreaming for you has been through prayer, meditation, or contemplation. But dreaming while awake is also different from how I was taught to pray. Rather than a petition to God, dreaming while awake is more like immersing yourself in a full sensory acknowledgement of a prayer that has *already* been answered. It is more like imagining with every sense of your body, soul, and mind's eye that you are having the experience you pray for, or dream of, or fantasize about now! The successful manifestation from this kind of prayer depends greatly on your ability to be immersed in every level of your being, not just in your thoughts, beliefs, and feelings; and this is where the Shaman's techniques play a vital and heretofore missing role.

What if in grade school, there was a period of time in the day when the teacher told the class to sit and daydream? Then what if the children were to write down or draw their daydreams on a piece of paper and put them in an envelope at the bottom of their dresser drawer for safe keeping only to open them up again perhaps months or years later? What percentage do you think might have come true? In a sense, this is what I am asking you to do in this book. And you will have the advantage of knowing why and how it works, and how to dream your world into being with a greater probability of success than ever before.

I think most of us have experienced uncanny coincidences, or synchronicities in our lives. For example, we have thought about a friend that we haven't spoken to in years, and seconds later they call. Or we tell an impressive story to a friend, and the following day, the friend experiences a similar event. Statistical probability simply cannot account for many of these events. I believe that these synchronicities occur because of the impact our clear thoughts and feelings have on the world around us, no matter the time or distances involved. Events are being orchestrated and set into motion at this moment from daydreams you are having today, to daydreams you will have a year from now. One of the most interesting validations of this concept that I've witnessed repeatedly comes from my clients who are actors. Unlike any other profession, an actor's work is to fully immerse themselves mentally, emotionally, physically, and sometimes to the depths of their soul into the characters they are playing. And this isn't just a short-lived daydream while the camera is rolling; instead, most good actors will "be in character" for weeks and months during the performance or shooting of the film. Invariably, these actors report that events and experiences in their own personal life begin to match those of the character and the scripts they are working on. Unfortunately, the drama that ensues in their real lives is not always what they prefer. My advice to these clients is that after the performance or shooting, they need to engage in a practice with the same level of dedication they give to their work, which resets their daydream back to the character and script they prefer to experience in their real life.

See if you can remember some of the events surrounding the coincidences or synchronicities in your life. Perhaps you deliberately dreamt of, prayed for, or spoke passionately about something that came true. I have found that the intensity of emotion, or how much something has impressed me, seems to have an impact on whether or not I experience a synchronistic event or dream come true. If you find this kind of correlation in your own experience, play with it a little and see what happens. Conduct your own scientific experiment. In the meantime come with me on this familiar journey, and I will share with you how easy and fun this dreaming the world into being can be. Together we will discover how powerful our conscious and deliberate daydreams can be with a little deeper understanding of how and why the process works and how we can do it most effectively. Then we will do it together for the world, tuck it away in our drawer, and see what happens.

Acknowledgements

I credit much of what is presented on these pages to my teachers, to my personal experiences throughout the world, and to all of the people I have had the privilege to know and work with over the last several decades. All of us learn from our own experiences and integrate many teachings into our personal knowledge base and toolbox, and we develop our own ideas and approach accordingly. I would like to acknowledge in particular Dr. Alberto Villoldo who provided me with the secret of finding the motivation to write a book by simply asking me to send him the first 30 pages; and, through sharing his comprehensive knowledge, teachings, and life experience, has been such a positive and profound influence on my life and work among the hundreds of thousands of others his work has reached. In addition, you may recognize in this book a great deal of influence from the Abraham-Hicks material, Ken Wilber, Greg Braden, and numerous others as the list continually grows. I am so grateful for all of these teachers and their wisdom, as well as for the deeply inherent wisdom that has come from just about every great tradition, Holy Scripture, teacher, guru, philosopher, scientist, writer, friend, and family member with whom I have dabbled, sometimes to great depths over the years. All of it starting with my mother and father, Marilyn and Bill, who handed me that first book by Richard Bach that opened my mind to endless possibilities, and who provided me with everything I needed to thrive, and most importantly with their living example of the greatest qualities any human can express. Likewise, I acknowledge my two brothers, Gregg and Bill, for setting the bar high, for their own deep faith, and for providing me with their endless love, teachings, and support, as well as my dear friend, Dr. Fred Ferrer, with his brotherly love, wisdom, and counseling. I would like to acknowledge my teachers and friends Dr. Geneie Everett, Dr. Richard Baldwin, Dr. Maura Cohen, Dean Hillyer, Shridhar, Zahir, Vianna Stibal, Linda Fitch, The Four Winds Society, and the Q'ero for their knowledge, wisdom, encouragement, support, and healing. For help in developing and editing the manuscript, and supporting my work in general, I wish to thank my dear friends Meg Withgott, Anasuya Krishnaswamy, Jo Bowlby, Louise Pearson, Jane Galer, Meeta Arcuri, Al Ballabio, Adam Hall, Lizanne Judge, Jodi Riviera, Brian Buchanan, Charlie Mitchell, Jodi Mitchell, Shannyn Riba, and Jennie Fairchild. I would also like to thank all of my colleagues and clients for their courageous journeys that have brought so much richness and inspiration into my life. And my greatest acknowledgement and gratitude goes to my wife, Gina, who naturally embodies and lives this work, and whose grace, beauty, wisdom, balance, humor, love, and friendship have kept my feet on the ground.

Lastly, and with great respect to all, I want to make it clear that the views, opinions, beliefs, and interpretations I express in this book are my own, and do not necessarily reflect the views, opinions, beliefs, and interpretations of my family, friends, teachers, clients, and employers. And although I've had the privilege of training with some of the most amazing people from around the world, I do not speak for, or claim to represent the teachers, indigenous cultures, healers, and shamans that I write about in this book.

Introduction

Throughout time, there have been select groups of people who have dedicated themselves to imagining new possibilities for the world. And by the act of fully immersing themselves into their vision, they have influenced the unfolding of those visionary dreams into reality. Throughout the ages, the techniques of dreaming the world into being have been the exclusive domain of elders, shamans, or monks from the world's most obscure societies, mystery schools, and religious organizations. Dreaming the world into being is a powerful process whose secrecy has been zealously hidden from the masses until very recently. Some of the information contained in the documentary "The Secret" and its popularity are a good example of how these guarded techniques have started to become more widely available. Since ancient times, those who have been privileged to information about this process have considered this type of understanding and power to be dangerous in the hands of the uninitiated. Perhaps this has been wise to some extent through the least conscious times in human history when ignorance and fear might have led to the wholesale abuse of these powerful techniques.

The rigorous initiations of these elite groups of visionaries were designed to clear away any personal agendas that may have been based on judgments, fear or greed, and old wounds, thus uncovering their true nature of love and compassion, and enabling the visions to more purely represent a benefit for all. But these days, more and more people at large have ready access to such information, spiritual practices, and healing professionals. This increased access has resulted in deep healing and an overall growth of awareness and consciousness. How many of your friends and acquaintances have become familiar with, and involved in, alternative healing, spirituality, and lifestyles over the last fifteen years? Have you noticed that you have been looking deeper into your Soul and psyche asking yourself more questions about what you are doing and why you are here? Are you finding greater levels of conscious awareness, love, and compassion stirring within you? I believe that those of you who have come to this book are ready, willing, and able to suspend any remaining personal judgments and fears, and to fully participate in this powerful act of taking Creation beyond where it has been before. In the words of the Sufi poet Rumi, "Out beyond the ideas of wrong doing and right doing, there lies a field… I shall meet you there."

My belief that we are now more than ever largely ready for this task of dreaming the world into being consciously and deliberately is supported by my personal experience as a healing professional. My belief is also supported by the prophecies and observations of the most sophisticated societies on the planet, such as the pre-Inka, Inka, Mayan, Hopi, Lakota, Tibetan, and Judeo-Christian. They all speak of this time when we return to our true nature as loving and compassionate beings, who are fully connected to our Source and to the Earth in harmony with all life. The Hopi call it the coming of the 5th world, the Inka call it the time of the 5th sun, the Mayan call it "Zero Tiempo," the Christians call it the return of the Christ, and the Jews call it the return of the Messiah. My teacher Alberto speaks of it as the birth of a new species called *Homo Luminous*.

In 2002, I was part of a small group that was privileged to attend the world prophecy reading of the master Q'ero shamans, called

Laika, who are direct descendants of the pre-Inka and Inka medicine people. The reading took place high in the Andes of Peru. The last time they had read their world prophecy was in 1995 and before that in 1945 when foresaw the coming of a new Golden Millennium, and before that over five hundred years ago when they foresaw the invasion of the Spanish Conquistadors. In the reading in 1995, they verified the significant Earth changes that they had first seen in their reading in 1945, and that are now happening due to global warming, such as the melting of the glaciers and the resulting drying up of their life giving lagoons. They also saw an increase in warfare as the old masculine warrior myths made their desperate last stand. And then they saw the next evolution of human consciousness into the way of allowing and peace.

Since the reading in 2002, the Q'ero have begun to do the readings monthly because they say that our prayers are working and that our new dreaming is impacting the world dramatically and positively. Just since I began working on this book in 2005, for example, mainstream business' across the globe have begun to embrace "going green" and are making sweeping changes towards sustainable practices across the manufacturing, production, and distribution cycle. One example is the behemoth Wal-Mart, who has hired the company of world-renowned environmentalist Adam Werbach to help them. Other multi-national companies with significant impact on the environment are consulting with the likes of Paul Hawken and Jib Ellison. Since the release of the documentary by Al Gore called "An Inconvenient Truth" in 2006, mainstream science, politics, and business have made an about face on protecting the environment astonishingly quickly.

Many of the Q'ero still live in small villages at 18,000 feet in the Andes, but are increasingly coming down to re-integrate into the mainstream villages of Peru. Since my teacher Alberto Villoldo started learning from them over 30 years ago, he has organized trips to Peru for his closest friends and students several times a year. The Q'ero walk the three-day journey out of their villages to meet these groups at sacred sites to share their wisdom, healing, and vision. These journeys are extraordinary adventures filled with not only the beauty of the land and people, but also with deeply powerful and transformational ceremonies.

For the prophecy reading in 2002, we met the Q'ero at an ancient pre-Inka site high above the sacred city of Ollyantaytambo, translated as the "resting place of the king." This is where the road ends and the Inka trail begins along the sacred valley of the Urubamba River, which is flanked by pure white glacial peaks reaching thousands of feet above into the dark blue sky. The Inka trail leads down the river to the ancient hidden city of Macchu Picchu at the edge of the jungle. We traveled up a connecting valley past the temple of the waters at Ollyantaytambo. We trekked across the terraces that run for miles up the valley from the river and up nearly a thousand feet along the slopes. My mind simply couldn't fathom how this ancient culture was able to carve out the hillside and move millions of tons of stone (some individual stones weighed as much as several tons each) across the rugged and nearly vertical terrain. The trail led us to the Pre-Inka temple ruins of Puma Marca, the "place of the puma," through small farms where people are still growing corn and living the same way that they have for tens of thousands of years. All along the way, we were greeted by the curious and smiling faces of the children, parents, and grandparents that find such peace and joy in taking care of the land that has been their true mother since the beginning of time.

When we arrived at the site, the Q'ero shamans were waiting for us and had already set up the ceremonial altar on the ground. They had effortlessly carried all of the supplies and healing stones for the altar on their backs. They prepared for a *Despacho* ceremony, which is a traditional Inka ceremony that returns offerings and prayers of gratitude to the Earth, heavens, and all of nature in its physical and non-physical forms. They gave the offerings in gratitude for all of the abundance they had already received—and all they knew they would continue to receive. Several thousands of feet above us, in caves amongst the rocky crags, lay the mummified bodies of their ancestors who had undoubtedly performed these same ceremonies for thousands of years, and whose spirit was still palpably with us. I remember placing my hands on one of the stone walls of the ruins, and having a vision of the people of this magnificent ancient culture welcoming us as equals.

After we made our offerings of sugar, corn, grains, lama fat, and prayers of gratitude into the Despacho, the Q'ero elders cleansed our luminous bodies by rubbing the gift over us while reciting prayers and repeating the Quechua word "picha," meaning cleanse. This cleansing process takes the heavy energies, or "hoocha," that we cannot process and gifts it to the Earth as well, because she can process it and turn it into life giving energy or "sahme," just as she does with our physical bodily wastes. After the Despacho ceremony, my energy level and clarity were noticeably heightened as we were prepared to hear the prophecy reading.

After much prayer and preparation, the elders consulted with the Great Spirit and with the conscious natural elements of the earth: the stone people, the plant people, the animals, the human spirits, and the planet spirits. The elders then deliberated and presented the prophecy with great nonattachment—and the same twinkle of joy in their eyes that I saw at our first meeting—as they expressed their delight that we magnificent Westerners would travel so far to see them. They clearly pointed out that the human species and planet as a whole is at a critical juncture and ready for an evolutionary leap. They said that the time was upon us to make choices right now that would determine if we can heal ourselves and the planet before a greater crisis forces us to. They said that those who lived with integrity, where their choices matched their desired outcome, would survive and thrive while others would have a difficult time. They mentioned that the great Earth changes they foresaw in their previous readings were well underway and that the next major crisis would arise from the actions of men that were living in fear and clinging to the old myths of victimhood and battle. They didn't offer much hope for the species as a whole, but emphasized that there was great hope for those making the choices to dream their ideal world into being and to match the dream with their thoughts, words, and actions.

Our current reality reflects this Q'ero prophecy with remarkable precision. To casual observers and scientists alike, there seems to be a tremendous amount of momentum towards crisis on a mass scale. My teacher Alberto says that twenty years ago, out of all of his acquaintances only a few were in crisis; but now, only a few are not in crisis. This crisis may take a multiplicity of different forms, such as the effects of global warming or Earth re-balancing (like hurricanes, floods, earthquakes and tsunamis), pandemic diseases from organisms that have mutated beyond the efficacy of modern medicine's biological war against them, internal psychological crises, or all out war against each other. However, there are other possible outcomes that lead to a world of greater harmony with each other and all of nature, abundance for all who desire it, and joy; and these outcomes also have momentum. So we have come to a time, right now, where the choices we make and the focus of our vision will tip the scale towards a greater manifestation of either of those experiences—harmony or crisis--in our reality.

This book is written for those of you who want to be part of the group of leading-edge visionary human beings. It is a practical guide for creating a world that until now would have been deemed highly improbable - if not impossible. And it is the calling of the author of this book to not only make the impossible possible, but to make it the most probable of world destinies with your help. My intent is ultimately to inspire anyone who comes in contact with my work to a life of greater power, freedom, and joy. In this book, I will explain Shamanism and the manifestation process, and provide the basic steps and helpful tools for this process, along with my own personal vision for the world.

Part 1
The Ancient and Modern Shamanic Knowledge and Visionary Process for Dreaming the World into Being

Shamans have been actively dreaming the world into being for millennia. As far as anyone knows, they were the first to actively and deliberately engage in this natural ability that is available to all. The focus of this book is to enable you to engage in this very dreaming process. As such, I will begin with a brief explanation of Shamanism and how it relates to the process of dreaming the world into being. In doing so, I hope to take the mystery out of Shamanism and all of the mystical and spiritual traditions that were built from it. Thus providing the keys to unlock the secrets and make them truly useful to all for the benefit of all. I think you will find that there is a little bit of shaman in all of us, and maybe quite a lot in your life. The tendencies to teach, to soothe or heal, to encourage and empower, to be a good mother or a good father, to serve, and to create are all a part of the characteristics of a shaman.

What is a Shaman?
Since the first humans began to walk the Earth and huddle in caves at night to stay warm and protected, there were always those who could see what others could not yet see. One of these visionaries was the first to notice the warmth around burning brush that had been struck by a bolt of lightning from the sky, and how it would spread from one piece of wood to another. She knew that she could gather that wood and that magic warmth from the sky and bring it into the cave to bring greater comfort to her family. Perhaps she was the first shaman. Or could it have been the person who first tossed a stone at a high hanging piece of fruit?

Surely, her family was amazed and delighted at the results of her vision and her ability to bring greater comfort and joy like no one had done before. Perhaps some were frightened by her magic abilities. Perhaps some were called to learn from her because they also had unique visions; and the first lineage of shamans was born.

Then there was the hunter that observed patterns in the migrations of the animals that no one had noticed before; and because of this, he was able to provide more good food for his family. Perhaps many were astonished at this one's ability to "speak" to the animals and know where they would be tomorrow. Perhaps they *did* speak to him, and give him the vision to observe and know their migratory patterns.

And another one wishing to improve the quality of life of her village, to see more comfort, joy, healing, and laughter, listened to what the plant spirits were telling her and extracted medicines from the plants. Or was it that she was intrigued by the sweetness of the water that the leaves had been sitting in, and noticed that it soothed her sore body or aching stomach? Whether it was the random firing of synapses in the brain that science may espouse, or direct dialogue with the Great Spirit, or both, the end result is all that really mattered to the people of the village.

Then there was the first storyteller, artist, and musician who noticed that she could soothe the children at night and bring teaching, laughter, and joy with her myths and performances. She would even don the skin of a deer to embellish the story, and paint great scenes and mythic images on the cave walls. Again, her people were amazed and delighted at the magic of this unique person, and again some would be drawn to learn and bring that same joy to others.

And as life and cultures became more complex, so these great lineages of shamans and their tools, techniques, and teachings grew in complexity. Throughout time, these people have been the ones who could connect with the unseen forces and bring new information and knowledge to improve the quality of life of those who were asking. They became the mediators of souls between the worlds. And more and more these shamans were admired, revered, and feared. Some continued to use their gifts to bring joy and wisdom to all that they could, seeing that this was good and that all the people could benefit and learn from it.

Some shamans began to relish the vision they had that others did not have, and began to realize that they could have power over them as a result. And they used their myths to increase that power and make it increasingly exclusive and secretive. Thus the spiritual cults and religions were born. There were also sorcerers who would use the Shamanic techniques as black magic to manipulate or do harm to others and attempt to gain more power, money, and infamy. However, theirs was not the power of love, healing, and creation, but instead a power based on fear, greed, and control.

With the advent of the religions, science, and spiritual cults, the ever evolving and open gifts of the shaman's vision and connection to the unseen became closed and permanently fixed in the pages of books, and guarded by swords. And those that feared the magic and words spoken by the hierarchy became the most easily controlled, while those that would find joy and learn from the

22

magic continued to do so, even within these structured and institutionalized forms of the Shamanic vision and wisdom. The leaders justified their approach, many with the original intent of bringing joy and a better quality of life. And so the religions, sciences, and spiritual cults continue to thrive to this day and do much service to the people, while others have experienced much disservice from them.

There have been times throughout history, when those practicing the institutionalized forms of Shamanism and sorcery have felt threatened by the original unstructured, open, and empowering forms of Shamanism, and have tried to destroy it. They had come up with many clever ways and myths to convince their followers that these empowering and life-affirming forms of Shamanism were non-serving, false, or indeed evil, and would lead to eternal suffering in and beyond this world. These sorcerers took advantage of people's fears, and whether by conscious intention or not, sorcery became an integral part of business, medicine, and politics as well as religions and cults. People would even inadvertently practice it on themselves through their own limiting beliefs, judgment, and guilt. In business for example, it is used to reinforce the kind of indentured servitude that is often required for corporations to succeed, or to convince people that success is measured by their ability to consume more and more products. In medicine, it is often used to sell more drugs, and inadvertently through diagnosis, which itself can become a self-fulfilling prophecy or life sentence. In politics, sorcery is used in many ways to gain favor, control, and power. These have been and continue to be the less pleasant chapters in the story of humanity.

Nevertheless, today there is an increasing awareness of the fear-based fallacies that have kept humanity from its greatest purpose and basis of life, namely joy and freedom, and the full expression of our true nature of love and compassion. People all over the globe are being reminded of the ancient and original intent of Shamanism, as well as the value and effectiveness of its open-ended teachings and techniques that continue to apply to even the most complex and modern of cultures. Science itself, through breakthroughs in Quantum Physics and Cosmology, is beginning to acknowledge and find proof for the very hypotheses that shamans have always relied upon and have already proven through the results of their work. Non-local phenomena, the relativity of time, the curvature of space, and the immeasurable and invisible "dark matter" and "dark energy" that science has concluded must make up ninety-six percent of the Universe, have always been the basic natural laws and phenomenon that shamans harness and apply.

And because of this increase in awareness, people are reconnecting to the gifts of both the unseen and seen forces of nature that are all around them, even in the big cities. People are reconnecting to the soul and spirit of all Creation in this way, and improving their quality of life like never before. Today's inventors, storytellers, artists, musicians, alchemists, mathematicians, scientists, medical doctors, psychologists, priests, and healers of all kinds are recognizing that they *are* the shamans of their villages, towns, and cities. In increasing numbers, they are seeking and completing full Shamanic training and bringing the comprehensiveness of the ancient wisdom teachings and techniques into their modern practices. And because of this, their intent to bring wisdom and joy to their people is being fulfilled more completely and with greater results than ever before. For, they are melding science and religion, the worlds of spirit and matter, the unseen and seen through the teachings and techniques of today's Shamanism. And the indigenous cultures who have held onto these Shamanic traditions throughout history and even through the most challenging of times, by sharing them once again with those who had forgotten, have created this trend that may actually bring the world and humanity back into balance; and not just that, but to an even greater level of joy, freedom, quality of life, and connection than ever before.

I use the word "shaman" because it is a simple and fairly universal title. The actual word comes from the medicine people of Siberia and has been widely adopted throughout the modern Western cultures to describe someone who facilitates a coming into power and freedom, which is often referred to as healing. Ideally, someone who practices Shamanism has been trained in techniques and initiated in a way that allows them to safely and effectively mediate between the physical and non-physical worlds in order to bring about some desired change on all four layers of our being: Literal/physical, Psycho-spiritual/mind, Mythic/subconscious, and Energetic/essential soul. While Western medicine diagnoses, maps, and intervenes only on the physical or psychological layers, the shaman engages the healing process on all four layers and preferably intervenes at the essential Energetic layer and then maps the new healed state at the Mythic layer. Shamans will stop the bleeding, set bones, prescribe herbs, and help change thoughts and beliefs, but they will also help empower you and help you to create more desirable experiences in the future, so that you no longer have to repeat the same old patterns and wounds that you or your ancestors have experienced in the past.

The shaman is a healer, a storyteller, a mythmaker, a wisdom keeper, a visionary, and a technician of the sacred that mediates between the worlds of energy and matter. Often through an altered or naturally different state of consciousness, she calls on all the forces of nature, both physical and non-physical, to help her do her work. She brings balance back into any situation by being in balance and dialogue with nature herself. Because of her preparation and relationship with the forces of the Universe, there is very little for her to actually do. She just has to be, and to hold a safe and non-judging space for the healing and visioning work to take place. The shaman sees no separation of matter and spirit, the way we do in modern Western and in many Eastern traditions. To the shaman, all matter is animated, and there is nowhere that spirit is not. For example, there is nothing more spiritual to the shaman than biology—how it seeks more complex and beautiful forms as atoms gather to form molecules, which then gather to form cells, which gather to form organs and eagles. And neither is there anything more spiritual than our man-made objects. It is all filled with spirit and consciousness.

The Work and Training of a Shaman

The shaman uses metaphor to describe her work. However, in contrast to how Westerners use metaphor, the shaman knows that behind the metaphor are both a real force that can be summoned and a process that can be engaged in to make real changes in the physical and Psycho-spiritual layers. An example of this use of metaphor is the four-step process of becoming a shaman that I have learned through the Four Winds Society, which follows:

1.　　　　The Way of the Healer. This is represented by the serpent who teaches us to shed the way we hold the wounds of the past the way she sheds her skin, which is all at once. This makes us available to power and knowledge. Even Western medicine has borrowed this metaphor by using the Caduceus (serpents wound around a staff and sprouting wings) and rod of Asclepius (serpent entwined around a staff) as symbols. The Shamanic process associated with the Way of the Healer is referred to as the Illumination process. An Illumination is like an Energetic enema that cleanses the chakras and luminous body and replaces the heavy energies with the light of our true nature. In the Way of the Healer, the shaman is connected, via initiation rites, to a lineage of healers (or *Hampe* in Quechua, the language of the Inka) that are the Earthkeepers from the past who assist us in our healing process. The shaman's luminous body is also given rites of protection, seeing, and harmony with the organizing principles and archangels of the three worlds: otherwise known in the West as the subconscious, conscious, and superconscious.

2.　　　　The Way of the Warrior. This is the way of the peaceful warrior represented by the jaguar, who teaches us to leap beyond fear and violence. Jaguar helps us to release old myths and stories that keep us bound to the same patterns that both we and our ancestors have been repeating - the patterns that inform how we live and die. With jaguar, we are able to clear ourselves of the way that death slowly stalks our spirit, taking our power until we are more dead than alive. Instead, we allow ourselves to be claimed by life and by our inherent power to create our own myths and follow our own footsteps, no longer needing to engage in battle the way our ancestors have, either internally or externally. The Shamanic processes associated with the Way of the Warrior are the

Extraction process, cutting Energetic cords, and the Death Rites (which are really the life rites). The shaman is connected through initiation rites to the lineage of the Daykeepers, or *Pampamesayoq* in Quechua, who are the bonesetters, midwives, herbalists, and keepers of the calendars and stone altars such as Stonehenge.

3.   The Way of the Sage. This is the way of the ancient wisdom and the wisdom to come that is passed down orally and through energetic transmission so that we can remember directly. This step is represented by the hummingbird, who teaches us how to reclaim our true nature and passion for life. Here we learn to manifest, appreciate, and be unattached. We shed our identities and teachers so that we have nothing left to defend and can now be truly free to create and work for the joy of it - drinking the nectar of life all along the way. Here we learn to enjoy the journey and the process of life including the contrasting negative or painful events, and we learn that the impossible can be made possible. This is the step where we stop having "spiritual experiences" because we are no longer physical beings having spiritual experiences, but instead we are spiritual beings having physical experiences. We learn to master time, to journey into the past and future in order to retrieve lost or compromised parts of our energy, to change our perception, and to nudge our destiny by re-aligning our energy with whom we desire to become. We also learn to keep a secret even from ourselves, so that life remains exhilarating – just like when you go to a movie and purposely keep the secret from yourself that the movie is just a script with a director and actors so that you can get fully into the drama. And finally we learn to be invisible, to blend in with our village in order to remain free and safe. The Shamanic processes associated with this step are the Soul Retrieval and Destiny Retrieval. The forces that the shaman

is connected to through the initiation rites in this step are the lineage of the Wisdomkeepers, or *Altomesayoq* in Quechua, who keep and share the wisdom teachings that come to us directly from the Source.

4. The Way of the Visionary. In this final step, the Eagle and Condor teach us to look at the big picture and be driven by a vision. We put the cart way before the horse, and use our creative power to dream a world into being for the benefit of our children's children. The Visionary comes from a place of total stillness and unity consciousness, and dares to make the possible more probable by tracking a vision well into the future. The processes associated with this step are to acknowledge what we have identified with, dis-identified with, transcended, and ultimately included as Creator. Here we do a lot of shadow work to dig deep into the subconscious in order to find and embrace that which may still be eluding us - secret battles that result in unwanted experiences and a waste of energy. We do this shadow work to ensure that our dreaming the world into being is done without the resistance of our own hidden judgments, projections, and personal agendas. The forces that the shaman is connected to through the initiation rites of this step are the lineage of the Earthkeepers, or *Kuraqaquyeq* in Quechua, who are the archangels and guardians of our galaxy.

Recently, two additional rites have been brought forth and passed on by the Q'ero Laika: the Starkeeper rites and the Creator rites. The Starkeepers, or *Maillku* in Quechua, are the stewards of the time to come - the next evolution of our species. This connection allows us to more easily process the contrasting events of our life at the essential layer instead of at the physical or psychological layers, so that our bodies actually react differently than before. For example, instead of reacting with the stress response of a flood of adrenaline and cortisols into our system, we can remain in a calm and balanced state.

The final rite of initiation called the *Taitanchis Ranti* in Quechua, or Creator rite, was introduced in June 2006 by the Q'ero Laika for transmission from human to human. This rite connects the shaman to the stewardship of all Creation in the Universe. This allows us to more easily realize our true Godliness and role in the creation process. This book is focused on the Way of the Visionary, the final step on the path of the power, freedom, and joy of creation.

Shamanism is profound, powerful, and at the same time very practical and pragmatic. The role of the shaman also includes showing up with a sense of the poetry and love of life, a kind of love that is not conditioned and is not judging. One of the greatest goals to a person of power, knowledge, and freedom is to live fully in the moment of now, to be fully present as opposed to preparing or waiting for the next experience to happen. I like to say that life is a series of moments, and you are either in them or not; similarly, life is a series of experiences that you either ask for deliberately and consciously or unconsciously. Can you remember those times in your life when you were fully in the moment, or as some would say, "In the zone", and when you were so focused on your goal that nothing could get in the way of achieving it? These are the moments when you are fully alive, or, as the shamans would say, being fully claimed by life.

You, Too, Can Be a Shaman
Most people would think of shamans as solely those medicine people of the indigenous cultures living on the outer edge of a

remote jungle, desert, or mountain village and born into a long line of healers. They often believe if that is not your story then you cannot be a shaman. I held that belief for years, and it kept me from realizing and fulfilling my destiny sooner rather than later when I was in my thirties. The truth is that those descended from such cultures are indeed the shamans/medicine people/healers of unbroken traditions and lineages going back as far as can be imagined, and thankfully they are still around. Some of these medicine people have maintained the powerful teachings and techniques learned, practiced, and expanded upon over hundreds of thousands of years, and are willing to help those who have forgotten and lost their connection to nature.

In terms of DNA, according to the groundbreaking work of Dr. Spencer Wells of the Genographic Project, all humans share common ancestors if we go back far enough in time. Even the "white" Northern Europeans are easily traced back to Asia, the Middle East, and ultimately back to Africa; and, the North and South Americans are traced back to that same ancestor in Asia and Africa. It has only been a relatively short period of time that the modern European cultures moved away from their nature-based mythologies, practices, and Shamanism. And as we shall explore later in the book, that separation can be traced to a very influential mythology and belief system that sprang from the first few pages of the Biblical translations and grew and spread across the planet over the last six-thousand years.

So the very good news for people who were raised in Western cultures and who now live in villages of millions, is that we are worthy and capable of remembering our true nature and of being shamans—if we so choose. And you can be a shaman, healer, and teacher without having to officially do the work that is labeled as Shamanic healing. It is more who you are than what you do. As I was discussing this concept with a friend of mine, he shared with me how one day as he sat in an office, he observed the window washer cleaning the outside of the office window. My friend was mesmerized and inspired by the grace, beauty, mastery, and total focus with which this window washer did his work. Similarly, my friend described his moments out on the river fly-fishing as his sacred altar with his fly rod being his wizard's wand or his Buddhist begging bowl. A good mother and good father are shamans. I have met what I would call shamans from nearly every walk of life, just based on who they are and the way they are in the world. In my case as well, I am just one of several thousands of Westerners who have made the choice to take the time and effort that is required to become trained and initiated to do the Shamanic healing work specifically. Many of my fellow students went through the same training without the intent of ever doing Shamanic healing on others, but simply to deepen their own inner work and to improve upon what they do for a living and what they experience in the world.

Everybody finds their inner shaman in different ways as well. I was raised in suburban settings as the son of a working-class family with two brothers. I was the youngest and followed mostly in the footsteps of my brothers. We all did well in school and sports and stayed out of any serious trouble. We went to church every weekend. My brothers went to notable colleges and ended up in good careers with families of their own. I followed suit with a degree in Electrical Engineering and worked for a decade in the high-tech industry of Silicon Valley. From all appearances, there was nothing extraordinary about my life. I did gather more experiences than my brothers did early in life by traveling the world with my work, and spending much time studying other cultures, philosophies, spiritual and Shamanic traditions, and other somewhat alternative pursuits. From my point of view however, this was just my insatiable curiosity and quest for knowledge, entertainment, and perhaps even some form of enlightenment at best. Some of these pursuits certainly set me up as the black sheep of the family or eccentric to some degree, but still nothing extraordinary seemed to occur in my life until the proverbial two-by-four hit me across the head.

As I began to read about, study, and practice more of the Eastern and esoteric mystical traditions, I recognized the reasons for some of my early life experiences. We could go all the way back to the day of my birth, which was two-weeks earlier than I was expected because everyone was crying and crushed as a result of the assassination of John F. Kennedy the day before. I also had the umbilical cord wrapped around my neck, and needed reviving. Then when I was about five years old, my family was visiting some friends who had horses. That morning I had spilled coffee on my shirt right over my heart. When we went out to bring carrots to the horses I reached through the pasture fence and managed to touch that wet spot onto the 10,000 Volt electric wire that is used to keep the horses in. As I returned to consciousness, I remember having traveled all over the place in what seemed like a very lucid dream-state. At one point, I was in front of my mom's face as she was in conversation, and later confirmed what she had been discussing. Then I was at what seemed like the ends of the Universe. During and for sometime after this near-death experience I felt that I knew everything. In fact, I became a very somber, calm, seemingly wise, and mature child beyond my years after that experience, and always seemed to have answers to questions about any subject. I even took to reading through an entire encyclopedia just for fun.

Subsequently, I had about five other near-death experiences mostly from car, motorcycle, and horse-related accidents. At the time of each incident, I didn't think much of it other than how lucky I seemed to be by coming out relatively unscathed. I just figured it was all a normal part of life until I learned later about the Shamanic death rites, the purpose of which was to become familiar with and map the non-physical worlds. These rights are done ceremonially, although the experience is every bit as real as a literal death without the trauma.

One other experience stood out that I later learned was equivalent to the Yogic tradition's rite of initiation called *shaktipat*. In *shaktipat* initiation, a learned master or guru who has attained a level of consciousness or enlightenment that a shaman would call total freedom and power or creator consciousness, passes a charge of energy and information to her student through a touch, a look, a mantra, a thought, or sometimes remotely through a picture or object. This act is said to open the student's chakras, or energy conduits, to be able to receive a greater level of knowledge and consciousness.

In my very early childhood up until age fourteen, I experienced daily migraine-like headaches from what I would assume was my sneaky diet of mostly sugar. The only way for me to find relief from the headaches was to practice a kind of transcendental meditation where I remained perfectly still and focused on one spot. When I was around sixteen years old and one year into a much disciplined bodybuilding regimen, I laid down one night on my waterbed the way that I normally would meditate myself to sleep. Just as I was dozing off to sleep, I felt a tremendous shock and flash of light go off in my head that was literally an explosion, as if I had been struck by lightning. My immediate thoughts and words to myself were that I had just died. I felt as if someone were standing to my left, and I looked over and saw nobody, but I did notice what seemed to be heavy steps walking across the ceiling and little gold sparkles of light as the steps moved from left to right across my room. Being the young Engineer in training, I first thought that perhaps my waterbed heating element had short-circuited, then I just thought to myself, "That was weird", and went to sleep forgetting all about the experience. About eight years later, I learned that this was a classic *shaktipat, or kundalini awakening,* experience.

Another interesting experience happened when my first martial arts teacher and I took a road trip together to Arizona and the Navajo reservation where we practiced the art of stalking that we had both read about in Carlos Castaneda's books. We spent the night out in the desert, and the following day I came down with the most serious illness I've ever had. It felt like how I've seen malaria depicted. It started with a tremendous weakness and shaking and high fever, and then I essentially lost consciousness for three days as my teacher stood by and waited. I didn't remember anything of those three days and took no food or water. When I came to, I felt absolutely great as if nothing had happened.

All of these near-deaths and other energetic experiences, as well as many other interesting events that I haven't touched upon here, happened before my mid-twenties. In my thirties, I met my first

Native American teacher, a medicine woman from New Mexico. She performed an initiation ceremony and gave me some powerful feathers, a bird wing, and a rattle and drum. I thought all of that was cool, and I had no idea what it was all for other than very generous gifts. She also guided me to take some more in-depth training in various healing modalities. My assumption was that all of this was just for my own healing. Similarly at age fifteen my brother's college roommate needed an adolescent subject for his Masters and Doctorate in Psychology and put me through an entire evaluation program. I simply thought it was great to have a friend like that who could later help me out with all kinds of advice and essentially free therapy as I went through the stages of life. I had no idea anything extraordinary was happening in my life, but it seems from hindsight that each of these events was leading up to that two-by-four that knocked me once and for all into the life I am living today.

In my early thirties, a family friend told me about an extraordinary healer named Dr. Richard Baldwin. I was told Dr. Baldwin could cure or heal just about anything, and that he had good psychic abilities as well. He was a chiropractor by official training, but self-taught in his ability to read and heal through information from his "guides" and a lot of muscle testing. He was a very nice, middle-aged, salt-of-the earth family man with a gentle and humble demeanor. I received sessions from him a few times, and his work did indeed solve some physical and relationship issues. In one particular session, I went in with the intent of gaining insight into what might be my most joyful career, as I was getting tired of the thankless fourteen-hour days of my high-tech job. He proceeded to tap into whatever psychic state he normally worked in and came back with the words "A mediator of souls between the worlds." I had no idea what it meant and just couldn't imagine that title written on a business card. He couldn't tell me what it was either, but he did say that something related to such work would come to my attention several times before I finally decided to pursue it. Over the next three years, I studied and started doing massage therapy on the side. I also began to take more workshops in alternative healing modalities, some of which were given by Western shamans like John Perkins and others. While most of the work was educational, fun, and powerful I didn't fully resonate with them in such a way that I could imagine doing their work for a living in my city.

Then one destined day, I walked into my favorite bookstore hoping to find something new and interesting and came across a book called "Shaman, Healer, Sage" by Dr. Alberto Villoldo. His picture was professional, even wearing a suit and tie, and the book read like a good Engineering manual including plenty of the poetry, story, adventure, and philosophy that I had grown to love. Everything in the book made logical sense and all the Shamanic healing steps that were presented seemed doable, even from a skeptical non-psychic's point of view like mine. Synchronistically, within two weeks of reading the book, I managed to secure the last spot in his workshop at Esalen Institute in Big Sur, California. I drove down the coast and on my way witnessed a condor flying next to my car, which to me was a good sign. When I arrived at the workshop I sat down next to Dr. Villoldo's seat in the circle, and one of the first things he said to me was that a shaman is just "A mediator of souls between the worlds." I was floored. I couldn't believe he had just defined the meaning of the exact words I had heard three years earlier. I asked Alberto if he thought I could do what he did, and without hesitation, he told me that I was already doing it and I just needed a little training. Within weeks after the workshop, I started the three-year intensive shaman's training program titled "Healing the Light Body" under the auspices of The Four Winds Society school that Alberto had founded.

From the beginning of my training, I experienced tremendous results in my own healing and the healing of those that I worked on. Although I never before considered myself psychic I discovered that if I simply spoke exactly what came into my thoughts it was surprisingly appropriate and effective for my client even if I thought it was just my imagination. After practicing Shamanism for over ten years now and doing thousands of Shamanic sessions, I am still unsure and always amazed at what takes place. Being the scientist and healthy skeptic that I am still, I always say if it ever stops working I'll find something else to do. I have seen many of my clients from all walks of life find their way into the Shamanic training as well. They too have experienced the powerful and tangible results that Shamanism brings to their lives and to the lives of people close to them. So don't be too surprised when discover your shaman within if you haven't already.

I remember one day early in my Shamanic training when I was with my teacher Alberto and about eighty fellow students. It was a serene and sunny day at a beautiful old monastery and retreat center in the foothills of Montecito, California. I was sitting outside of the old church where we were holding our class. It had been an intense day of healing work for me, which was compounded by the fact that having been raised Catholic there was something a little unsettling about training to be a shaman in front of the religious altar of my childhood. The old feelings of obligation, self-judgment, unworthiness, and guilt had been surfacing strongly. One of my classmates was an elderly woman who had spent most of her adult life as a nun; so we were all steeped in questions of identity, reconciliation, and belonging as she expressed her feelings, which were very similar to my own. The whole scene was so surreal that I found myself in somewhat of a dream state.

I was sitting alone at an outside table during a short break from the intense training schedule. I had many questions running through my head, but was welcoming the break and the opportunity to make a fan out of some hawk feathers and a stick the way my Northern Native American teachers would. I think it was my way of finding a connection to a lineage that was not a part of my history or ancestry in this life. My thoughts were filled with questions of who I was and who I could or couldn't be. At one point Alberto came over to the table and sat down. I was so intent on making the fan that I barely looked up to say hello, squandering a valuable and rare opportunity to converse one-on-one with my teacher. Perhaps I was silenced by the thoughts of unworthiness and hierarchy spilling over from the priests and teachers of my past, and projected them onto my current role as a student of Shamanism. Alberto does not subscribe to any hierarchical classification, and therefore considers me a brother. He attempted to connect with me by asking about the feathers. I don't think I even looked up while I gave him a short answer and stayed focused on my handywork. About a minute of silence passed, and Alberto got up to leave and said to me in a very kind and warm tone "Don't confuse the work with becoming an Indian," and he disappeared before I looked up.

Alberto's lesson hit me like a Mack truck in that moment. From that point on I wasted no energy trying to be something I could never be—and didn't need to be—and focused my energy on how I could serve most with the work. One year later, I was standing in an airport in Peru getting ready to part ways after an incredible month-long expedition with Alberto and the Q'ero shamans that was filled with powerful experiences and personal healing. Alberto mentioned to me what a beautiful and successful journey it had been. Without hesitation and from a place of deep knowing, I replied that now it was time to go home and get back to my clients and "grow corn" with my experiences. The information he had passed to me a year earlier had become knowledge. Alberto had taught me how to serve my experiences, rather than be served by them.

Becoming a Modern World Shaman
Alberto says that it is important that we all find the shaman within—our own deep connection with our true nature, knowledge, and power—and that traveling around the world with the natives is not necessary to find it. It may be right there in your own backyard, so to speak, and in the culmination of your own experiences, study, and knowledge. Through a synthesis of over twenty years of study of traditions from around the world, the core of my Shamanic practice has its foundations in the teachings, rites of passage, and techniques of the Q'ero Indians of Peru as they were brought to me primarily through Alberto's synthesis and adaptation. I found that Alberto's teachings contained a complete collection of all that I had learned elsewhere and then some; and, I find it important that new teachings harmoniously build upon what has made sense and worked before.

As a Medical Anthropologist and Psychologist, Alberto studied the indigenous cultures of the Americas starting in Alaska, working his way down the continent, and ending up in Peru. He found Peru to be exceptional in that about 97% of its population of approximately thirty million people are Indios still living in the wild, so to speak, while the "white people" live in the "reservations"—the big cities like Lima. He contrasts this to the approximately 1.8 million Northern Native Americans who remain from the 100 million who once thrived in a sustainable way in the United States. These Native Americans were also heavily affected by Westerners in ways similar to the experiences of many of the world's indigenous cultures who have survived attempted genocides, from today going back to the Celtic destruction by the Romans nearly two thousand years ago and to earlier cultures and periods in history.

Alberto recognized an opportunity to learn ways that have been largely untouched for over 50,000 years because the Q'ero shamans in their centuries of isolation seemed least influenced by the Western cultures. He was the first Westerner to have contact with the Q'ero, and when he described them to his Anthropologist colleagues, they quickly dismissed his claims since they "knew" that the Inka had been extinct for centuries. With quick thinking, Alberto encouraged them to continue to write that the Inka were extinct in their journals so that the Q'ero and their culture would not be quickly swallowed up and lost into the limited annals of Western science.

Alberto has spent over thirty years living and studying with the Q'ero in the Mountains, high plains, and jungles of Peru. He currently works with the Q'ero to help them to re-integrate into society and is continually evolving his knowledge and teachings. With his time, dedication, and ability to bridge the Q'ero techniques and world-view with the best of the Western healing sciences, Alberto created a comprehensive program of initiation, self-healing, teaching, and healing practices. Thousands of students from around the world learn the techniques and receive the rites that connect them to a lineage of healers and shamans going back to time immemorial and forward to a time to come. Moreover, many travel and learn directly from the Q'ero master shamans, or *Laika*, several times a year.

Recently Alberto's work has expanded into other neighboring Shamanic cultures that, similar to the Q'ero, are coming forward and reintegrating into the mainstream modern world. One such culture is that of the women shamans of Chile known as the Machi. They are the direct descendents of the Mapuches natives who were able to defend themselves against invasions by the Inca, the Spanish Conquistadors, and the modern-day religious missions. Like the Q'ero, their worldview and techniques have been maintained in a pure form for tens of thousands of years. The Machi shamans are highly respected and now fully integrated into the modern Chilean healthcare systems working side by side with Western trained doctors.

My Shamanic practice, like Alberto's teachings, includes other techniques and wisdom that I have found to be effective for my "village": the high-tech, fast paced, professional, and highly complex life of big city America. This adaptability illustrates one of the great beauties of Shamanism, which is that it is an open and continually evolving system. And beneath the surface still runs the foundation of my religious upbringing, as well as years of study and practice in many other religions, philosophies, spiritual practices, and Western sciences. I have incorporated these traditions with all of their beauty, richness, and healing, as well as the strengths that result from healing old wounds. This foundation allows me to resonate with and speak to the wide variety of clients that come my way. Now is the time for healers and teachers to find the common threads that run through every tradition and that most effectively address the needs of the people that come to them.

Pre-Inka, Inka, and Post-Inka Shamanism and Prophecy
The story of the Q'ero is a fascinating one. The Q'ero had isolated themselves for the last 500 years since the time when the Western culture of the Spanish Conquistadors made its way to Peru in search of gold. Just before the arrival of the Conquistadors with their horses, armor, and guns, the Inka medicine people and prophecy keepers read the signs of half-men and half-beast with skins of steel and thunder sticks coming to turn the Inka world upside down. They called this the Pachakuti, which translated from the Quechua language literally means earth (Pacha), turned upside down (kuti).

Since our view of the world is largely based on our mythologies, what the Pachakuti meant was that the Spanish were bringing a mythology with them that was nearly opposite or upside down compared to the Q'ero. For example, to the Q'ero, the feminine mother earth gave birth to the masculine as it does in all of nature. They lived in harmony with nature and all creatures as stewards of the earth, or caretakers of the garden so to speak, where not only do the minerals, plants, and animals feed them, but they also have much to teach by way of their characteristics and instincts. In addition, they believe that creation is an ongoing

43

process, and that there is no greater act of love and power than to participate in creation by dreaming the world into being.

In stark contrast to the indigenous worldview, the Spanish claimed that the feminine was born from the masculine (Adam's rib) and that humans were cast out of the Garden and given an antagonistic relationship with nature (original sin and thorns and thistles) and the feminine since it was Eve tasting of the fruit of knowledge that caused the punishment. They further claimed that Creation was finished in six days and is now closed, and there is nothing we can do about it except battle for limited resources or hope to inherit the Earth at the end of time. This has formed the basis of our masculine warrior dominated modern world and the philosophies and psychologies of redemption.

The Q'ero immediately recognized that a worldview based on an antagonistic relationship with nature and our bodies, where the feeling body is considered the feminine in both men and women, and where the logical mind is considered the masculine, would not work very well. The mythic stories of why and how we are here on the Earth and what it all means have a powerful influence on our belief systems and our perceptions, both conscious and unconscious, and largely dictate our thoughts, actions, reactions, and experiences. To the Q'ero, it was an obvious observation and an inevitable outcome of the Western myths that a battle with "mother" nature could only lead to environmental disaster, war, and disease. And so the Q'ero retreated to the mountains to hold onto the feminine-based myths that lead to harmony and well-being.

The Next Pachakuti or "World Turning Over"

The Q'ero tell us that they have come back from the mountains at this time to help Westerners to get back to the Garden as soon as we can before our situation gets worse or ends apocalyptically. They say that we can wait until the "end of time" for the return of the Messiah, or the return of the Christ, or instead we can do it today. We can bring the Messiah or the Christ to Earth now. We can taste the "fruit of the second tree and become as creators" and bring Heaven on Earth today. They understand how we create by the principle known as "ask and it is given." They know that we cannot judge because our minds are not capable of seeing the whole picture. They recognize that they are not only growing corn but also growing Gods by helping us to remember our true nature and abilities.

It was less than sixty years ago that the descendants of those original Q'ero came down from their villages and made themselves known to the rest of the world. Even the Peruvian Indians thought that these people were only the stuff of legends and lore. The Q'ero shamans decided to return because their prophecies spoke of another *Pachakuti*, this time led by the "round-eyed" Westerners that would bring the world back into harmony. This new *Pachakuti* will allow us to return to the Garden and evolve from the current paradigm of fearful victim consciousness into creator consciousness. They refer to this new human being as *Homo Luminous*; and becoming a *Homo Luminous* is equivalent to becoming an angel, or Bodhisattva, or obtaining Christ consciousness. And so they began to teach us how to make this evolutionary leap as quickly and gracefully as possible. Alberto's teacher, Don Antonio, would tell him that he has a dinner engagement with Great Spirit, that he needs to go back to the Garden and taste the fruit of the *other* tree - the tree of everlasting life that would allow him once again to be creator and no longer victim.

Don Antonio also emphasized the importance of the role that the children who are coming into the world at this time are playing in this evolutionary step. There is a significant amount of information that has been published about the unique qualities of many of the children who have been born over the last thirty years or so. Those doing the work on the leading edge of this phenomenon refer to these children as *Indigo Children*, or more recently, the *Rainbow Children*. Mainstream Science and Medicine has been grappling with a parabolic rise in "diseases" such as Attention Deficit Disorder (A.D.D), or Attention Deficit Hyperactivity Disorder (A.D.H.D), and Autism. Within my shamanic experience of these children, I recognize that the underlying foundation of their symptomatic "diseases" is a function of the difficulty that they as the new humans with their heightened awareness, intelligence, and sensitivity are having with a world that seems not yet ready to fully support them. The main part of Don Antonio's life and message, included in his final words to Alberto, is that for the sake of the children we adults must do our healing quickly, and we must evolve ourselves now in order to support this new evolution of the species. Do you know any of these children? If so, I would encourage you to ask them what it is that they have come to teach us.

The Shamanism of the Q'ero

The Shamanism of the Q'ero is non-hierarchical, non-institutionalized, and un-written. It is an open system that is still evolving along with us. Being non-hierarchical means that if I come up with a more effective technique and tell one of the elder Q'ero Laika about it, she'll say, "Great, teach me!" Being non-institutionalized allows our energy to remain focused solely on the work itself, with all we have in front of us at the moment of now, as opposed to draining energy in the preservation of an institution and its doctrine. Being un-written allows the tradition to remain in the present, and to flow and evolve with Creation itself. In addition, being un-written means it is not only an oral tradition, but also a direct transmission of the timeless knowledge and wisdom from the Source. These transmissions occur in ritualistic initiation rites from forehead to forehead and from stone altar to stone altar creating energetic threads that connect us through time and space. They form a luminous network of a powerful team of both physical and non-physical healers and teachers that are present whenever a client asks for help or whenever we engage in dreaming the world into being.

My View of Shamanism
Shamanism is practical in that its goal is to obtain results in our physical reality, which is considered the leading edge of Creation. Our experiences of the physical world make up the theater of Creation where there is drama and the contrast of pleasure and pain. Without contrast there is just monotony - the one blank nothingness or Void. Ideally, our time here in the theater is filled with more pleasure than pain, and when the pain is too great, it is helpful to remember once again that we are spiritual beings having a biological experience. But ultimately we are here to be physically focused and to play and relate in this world of contrast. For example, my teachers say that it is great to have a mystical, spiritual, or mind-altering experience, but then how do you grow

corn with it? Otherwise, it just makes for interesting conversation over the dinner table.

Simply put, the goal of Shamanism, as I practice it, is to most quickly, safely, efficiently, gently, elegantly, and gracefully bring my clients and myself into greater freedom, power, and joy. This increased freedom allows us to fully uncover our loving and compassionate nature and to create more of the life experiences that we would prefer. We can be free to choose greater connection, clarity, understanding, material abundance, love, support, physical and mental well-being, fulfillment in work, relationships, and all other aspects of life, or we can equally choose more suffering, pain, and bondage. And my teachers would say all of that is spiritual as well since there is no separation of spirit and matter; there is only the natural Universe and its visible and invisible components. There are healing modalities that address all levels of our being that do not use the word shaman, but I personally refer to them as Shamanism or Shamanic in their nature. So where many specific paths in a forest may each have individual names, scenery, and beginning and ending points, I like to view my Shamanic practice as the whole forest.

There are also many approaches to Shamanic traditions from various ancient cultures and modern schools. The various approaches have their own frameworks, sets of beliefs, metaphors, and techniques, but are remarkably similar at their core. Much like various schools of modern medicine will teach different approaches and techniques to treating a disease or conducting a surgical procedure, but in the end share the same goal. And since anatomy and physiology is universal across the Earth, the core methods and outcomes are very similar. Likewise, many shamans have specialties and certain approaches that appeal to and resonate with their particular specialty more so than other approaches. Thus, I find it helpful to remember the big picture and recognize the beauty of the entire forest with all of its paths.

Shamanism Versus Sorcery

It is important to clarify the difference between a shaman and a sorcerer because they are often confused. A sorcerer also works with unseen forces to influence change just as the shaman does. The key difference is that a shaman deliberately chooses not to practice sorcery, that is, not to disempower another for the sake of gaining power for themselves or their clients. The sorcerer is for hire to either help or harm, while the shaman is dedicated only to helping and empowering her clients and others.

Interestingly enough, the most prevalent use of sorcery is self-sorcery based on our limiting beliefs, fears, and self-judgment. If you suspect that someone is practicing sorcery against you, just know that it can only get to you where fear lives within you; therefore, the greatest protection is to heal yourself and come into the power that is your birth-rite in the first place. The ultimate solution is to move from victim consciousness to creator consciousness. You may want to explore any areas of your life where fear is the motivating factor. When my client is faced with an important decision, I have them make two columns on a piece of paper, one labeled Love/Joy, and one labeled Fear. Then as they come up with the various questions and scenarios related to each choice in their decision process, I have them determine under which column each belongs – Is it a love/joy-based choice, or a fear-based choice. For example, when faced with the decision to accept a new job offer or not, are they thinking that if they do not accept they may be missing out on a great opportunity for security, money, or advancement? Or, are they thinking they would have fun being involved in a particular project related to the new job if they do accept, or rather more fun with the other choice if they do not accept the new job? The first belongs under the column of Fear, and the latter under the column of Love/Joy. This exercise can be applied to all areas of you life, and will help you to become aware of where the fear lives within you, so that you will not be susceptible to self-sorcery or the sorcery of those who might influence your decisions. My recommendation is to make the choices based on love and joy.

I was once referred a potential client I will call Nancy. She had already worked with several psychics and healers but was not getting the desired results. For about an hour I listened to her story and to what she had gleaned from the psychics. In summary, her ex-husband, whom I will call Ken, was seeing another woman who seemed to be controlling him in such a way that Nancy could no longer trust his intentions and did not feel comfortable when he was caring for their two year-old daughter. Because Nancy was highly experienced in spiritual practices, she felt that the situation had nothing to do with her, and that even Ken was not creating it intentionally. She was convinced, and supported in her belief by a psychic reading, that the other woman had hired a sorcerer to control Ken and destroy whatever was left of their relationship. She was firmly seated in the fear-based victim consciousness approach.

What Nancy wanted was a good relationship with Ken and possibly even getting back together. At the very least, she wanted a relationship that would allow them to raise their daughter together even if separated. She asked that I stop this other woman and get her out of Ken's life. What Nancy was looking for was a sorcerer to battle the supposed other sorcerer. I explained to her that I don't practice sorcery but that I could work on her so that she would be in her power enough to create the relationships she really wanted for her and her daughter, whether it had anything to do with Ken or not. And if a sorcerer was working against Ken, then I could work directly with him and empower him against the sorcery, but only if he chose. Otherwise, it would just become a battle of sorcerers; and most battles end in draws after a lot of damage has occurred; and shamans ideally don't engage in battle in the first place. It could also have been that the other woman might have truly believed she was protecting Ken from Nancy.

The bottom line is that regardless of how right and enlightened a person thinks they are, to try to control another person's life to further one's own agenda is sorcery, and based entirely on the notion that we can judge. This fear-based approach is firmly rooted in the victim-perpetrator-rescuer triangle that keeps us trapped into playing any one of those roles at any given time. Nancy's situation was a clear example of this.

I performed Shamanic-healing sessions with Nancy, Ken, and their two-year-old daughter. The truth of the whole situation turned out to be far from Nancy's original story and perception. Nancy's troubles stemmed mostly from self-sorcery and misunderstanding that came from Ken's fear of being judged by Nancy and the ensuing punishment he would receive from her. This fear was keeping him from being completely honest about his desire to be with the other woman whom he truly loved. In summary, the result was that Nancy learned what was really happening and healed the old wounds so that she could release Ken and attract a new relationship that would support her in the way she wanted, and be a good example for her daughter. Ken healed his old wounds and felt safe enough to speak his truth, and their daughter stopped having nightmares. The best part was that none of them would have to repeat this scenario again as the deep Shamanic healing removed the source of the original pattern.

Another form of sorcery, even if it is well intentioned, is the sharing of a diagnosis. Many a healer will go to great lengths to diagnose and convince someone that they need to take action to be cured or healed, even chasing them down on the streets to tell them this. Diagnosis is of course helpful to treat an acute situation that has fully manifested and may be life threatening in order to bring comfort and buy more time for the healing process. The problem is that a diagnosis itself may "lock-in" the condition when told to the client, and furthermore, the person may not be ready or wanting to be healed or even cured. Shamans move very quickly beyond diagnosis because to them any "illness" is just part of the story and the mechanism or manifestation of the deeper Energetic wound that ultimately needs to be healed.

I like to say that a person can't hear the answer to a question they haven't asked. Therefore, it is important for the healer to allow a person his or her own timing and wait until someone asks for healing, and then to stay away from the story or diagnosis. Anything other than that may be considered sorcery. To clarify for the sake of my Western doctor friends, diagnosis is not necessarily harmful as long as the patient can change his or her perception of it. And diagnosis is clearly necessary for the treatment of acute conditions that have manifested and need to be addressed in the physical reality. Nonetheless, after the doctor has stopped the bleeding or removed the cancer cells, shamans would prefer to engage in the healing at the level of the Energetic source or soul – the very blueprint or template of our existence.

As another example from my work as a massage therapist, I have witnessed the inadvertent practice of diagnosis-type sorcery. Often during a massage, the client will ask or make the comment that they have many knots or that their muscles are extremely tight. The well-intentioned therapist will often collude responding "Oh yes, this is very tight," and they might even go on to talk about all the stress in the client's life and how many other illnesses it can cause. The therapist thinks that raising the client's awareness to their issue will help them learn and make changes, which may eventually happen, but it is usually unlikely without follow-up. A non-sorcery response would be something like "Your muscles feel normal," or "Relatively speaking, you are doing well," and most importantly, "Your muscles are responding very well [to the massage]" or "They are really loosening up." Some may call this the power of suggestion or hypnosis, but when it is applied with the intent of serving the desire of the client, it is a healing or Shamanic approach as opposed to sorcery.

Shamans and Saints
Another important point about shamans is that they aren't necessarily "saints" either. Shamans are not attempting to completely transcend those aspects of being human that we've been taught are negative, such as anger, fear, grief, and ego. The shaman understands that these are all essential and even useful aspects of physical life here on the planet, and they will always be

a part of who we are. The difference lies in approaching and using these parts of ourselves from a place of power and freedom, so that they serve us rather than control or harm us. I like to use the story of Jesus in the temple when he got very angry and toppled the moneychanger's tables, having fully expressed his anger and then fully released it within minutes. Furthermore, without the use of ego Jesus would not have been able to create a huge following— one that has lasted 2000 years. These are just two examples of the many that can be found in the lives of well-known prophets and saints of all religions. So, while we are all naturally loving and compassionate at the core of our being when we are completely free of fear and all the contrasting aspects of fear, it is an appropriate part of the drama and diversity of life to contain and express all aspects.

In my experience, it is the notion that we are *supposed* to become perfect saints, and the ensuing self-judgment, that causes most pathologies and problems in the human species. First, we beat-up on ourselves for not fulfilling some arbitrary notion of what it is to be a perfect human being; then, as soon as we think we've attained some level of clarity, we judge and beat-up on others to get them to agree with us. This is what I call the self-righteous trap. These internal and external battles lead to tremendous imbalance and suffering. If you were to closely examine the life of anyone who has been deemed a saint, then you would see that it is our mistaken notion that they are anything but as fully human as the rest of us. Much like the celebrated saints, shamans strive for more allowing, gentleness, and compassion for all that we are, and the knowledge that unconditioned and non-judging love is the answer.

Transcending those aspects of humanness that would normally control us for the sake of coming into power, freedom, and joy is a fine goal, but don't forget to go back and use those valuable aspects of human experience. Ken Wilber refers to this process of Psycho-spiritual development as "transcend and include." He says that as we go through the stages of development, we transcend each previous stage, but they remain an essential part of our being; and to deny this leads to various forms of dysfunction. For example, in biological evolution, a molecule transcends the atom, and a cell transcends a molecule, but each must include and embrace its previous stage of existence.

Another very insightful point related to our stages of development, comes from the work of Dr. Clare W. Grave and is known as Spiral Dynamics. I find it critical to understand this model in order to overcome judgment. Put simply, whatever stage of development you are in at any given time, you naturally consider it to be the highest attainable and all of your perceptions are colored by your particular stage. So if another person comes along who is more developed, being obviously different from yourself, you assume that they are not at your stage and therefore must be at a lower stage of development. Because of this, you may confuse the teacher with the teachings, and reject both essentially throwing the baby out with the bathwater. This is most clearly illustrated by the predominance of persecutions of those people that we later consider some of our greatest prophets, visionaries, and teachers from Jesus to Galileo to Joan of Arc. Shamans work around this issue by changing perceptual states or shapeshifting to match the stage of whomever they are working with. They do what they can to avoid being placed on a pedestal so that their student or client keeps their attention on the teachings. Alberto calls this being so seen or transparent that you are invisible. So the client will neither persecute nor worship the shaman, and, thus stay empowered and focused on following his or her own footsteps.

The Value of Childlike Innocence

I don't consider myself an expert on any of the topics that I cover in this book. So you may not find a comprehensive, heavily researched study of what the historical and current situation is relative to each topic, or educated predictions of what is to come; you can already find plenty of published material for that level of detail. Instead, you will find a simpler vision from me, unfettered by too much information, but filled with much intuition, heart's desire, and sometimes way out of the box of conventional "wisdom." I have found in past experience that an intuitive or even naive approach often leads to quick and elegant solutions that the experts couldn't see. For example, my teacher Alberto tells a relevant story of the elder shamans. If they are facing a very daunting healing, they will bring in the youngest and least experienced shaman to facilitate it because she doesn't yet know that it is nearly impossible or has never been done – and because of this naiveté, the "impossible" healing happens. So in this book, I'm bringing my lack of expertise and my eager and positive outlook to the table.

The Value of Maintaining Diversity and Room for Change

Another point I'd like to emphasize is that my viewpoints and vision may also seem overly simplified; and that is okay because this isn't about solving all of the world's problems, nor is it about getting rid of any of the contrast and creating some kind of panacea for every situation and every living creature. There will always be tremendous diversity and it will continue to grow. The important thing is to know that you can deliberately and consciously choose the parts of the diversity that you would like to see grow in your own experience.

The interesting thing about putting these ideas in written form is that once it is written and published, you can't un-write or un-publish it. This creates a dilemma for me since I learn as I go and often change my ideas or perspective. Ever since reading Ralph Waldo Emerson's essay "Self Reliance" in high school, I no longer place a premium on consistency. He wrote, "A foolish consistency is the hobgoblin of little minds, adored by philosophers, statesmen, and divines. ... Speak what you believe today in words as hard as cannonballs, and speak what you believe tomorrow in words equally hard even if it contradicts everything you say today." You can imagine how compelling and unforgettable words like that are to the mind of a sixteen-year-old; and they are still music to the ears of a shaman.

"You Should Have Stayed a Catholic"
I now understand more fully why Shamanism is an un-written teaching—it has to be in order to remain an open and evolving system. This is why I encourage you to read this book as an inspiration towards the development of your own vision and understanding and not as a "gospel" according to Jon because by the time you read this Jon's take on it will surely be different in some way and hopefully expanded and clearer. Also, as much as I enjoy working as a shaman and presenting these ideas and visions, because I've been asked to and feel it is of service, I remain open to the possibility that I could be entirely out in left-field. I often tell my clients that despite all that I'm offering and how confidently I'm presenting it, I want them to follow their own

inner guidance, gut feelings, and footsteps—even if it continues to be the footsteps of their religious or spiritual leaders. With a bit of a smile I like to say that I'm open to the possibility that when I die I will actually go to the pearly gates and St. Peter will say to me "You blew it, you should have stayed a Catholic." I truly think it is important to stay uncertain enough so as not to create another religion or cult, and the self-righteous judgments, missions, inquisitions, and battles that tend to result.

An Uncanny Ability to Foresee Future Trends
And one final note on why I think this journey together will be fruitful. I have noticed throughout my life that I'll be very interested in or into some new concept years before it becomes mainstream. For example, I remember reading about and practicing the Chinese art of Feng Shui when there was only one book about it at the local New Age bookstore. Ten years later, there were many books, and everybody was a Feng Shui consultant. When I was fourteen years old, I was wholeheartedly into nutrition and exercise, even working at a local spa as a trainer. Some years later everyone was going to the gym and reading books and getting video tapes and having personal trainers; and the same thing happened with Tai Chi, massage, yoga, diet, and environment, to name a few. And now it is Shamanism. In fact, recently the Washington Post asked my teacher Alberto to do a full-page article on Shamanism. When he asked why, they said that "Shamanism is no longer a fad, it is a trend." And through dreaming and the subsequent synchronicities, I'm now practicing Shamanism in a spa at a five star resort, and I won't be surprised to find these services offered at many spas and all other mainstream healing venues in the not too distant future. So you might say that this book represents the first time in my life where I've

acknowledged my visionary gift and decided to really share it on a grand scale and grow corn with it. If this phenomenon continues, I truly believe our vision for the world will manifest as well.

Chapter 1
Opening Sacred Space

Since reading this book is an act of power and knowledge, it is appropriate to open sacred space as all the people of power and knowledge do before a great act like nudging destiny. Creating sacred space for Shamanic work is analogous to a surgeon making sure the operating room environment is sterile before she cuts open your body. The energetic mirrors the physical, and the sacred space creates an energetically safe environment to reorganize the luminous architecture of our energy bodies. Just as plants, animals, minerals, sunlight, moonlight, starlight, air, and water feed our bodies so that we can be here physically and play, they also help us mythically and energetically. The shaman, having never left the Garden, is easily able to call on all these nonphysical forces of nature to come and hold the space. Imagine that these forces are eagerly awaiting your call, like a good old friend who hasn't heard from you for a while.

It is said that the shaman has only one contract and it is with Spirit. The contract states that when the shaman calls, Spirit comes immediately and unconditionally. The fine print of the contract also states that when Spirit calls, the shaman comes immediately and unconditionally. These extra-psychic forces of nature are both archetypical and very real and they show up in many ways. When a shaman begins to engage with these forces it is said that they are not only the stalker of power but are also being stalked by power, and sometimes power shows up at five in the morning before you've had your coffee and shower and grabs you by the scruff of the neck saying, "Let's go!"

The beauty is the unconditional love and support that these forces bring us to improve the quality of our life. Thus, as part of the calling of these conscious energies, we honor them by acknowledging what they do for us. When we complete our work, we again acknowledge and thank them as we release them. This helps us to feel that we are in a good reciprocal relationship with them; what the Q'ero call "ayni." The following is offered as a guideline for opening sacred space, and should be read aloud or silently while facing each direction, beckoning with your open hand. Burning sage, using a rattle and drum, or spraying flower water with your breath can accompany the prayer to enhance the clearing of any energies that do not belong in the space around you.

"To the Winds of the South - Sachamama, hatun Amaru,
Great Serpent. Mother of the waters, the rivers, the galaxies, and the roads that bring us together, come wrap your coils of light around us.
Teach us to shed the energies of the past that no longer serve us, the way you shed your skin, which is all at once.
Show us how to walk softly on the Earth, in the beauty way, so that all we touch and create, we touch and create in beauty.
Ho!

To the winds of the West - Otorongo, Mother Sister Jaguar.
Come protect our medicine space, and devour those energies that do not belong to us.
Teach us your ways beyond fear, anger, death, guilt, shame, and all the mythologies, stories, and beliefs that no longer serve us.
Help us to be impeccable, luminous beings, peaceful warriors who have no need to engage in battle internally or externally, but

instead are able to support ourselves in asking for and receiving the core experiences we truly desire so that we can leap into who we are becoming and create from a place of love.
Ho!

To the winds of the North - Grandmothers, Grandfathers, Ancient Ones, Ancestors and Guardians of this Land.
Come to us and teach us your ancient wisdom and the wisdom to come, we honor you who have come before us and will come after us – our children's children.
Help us to remember that ancient wisdom directly and take our seats with you that we have never really left. Come warm your hands by our fires, and whisper to us in the winds. Siwarkenti, hummingbird, teach us to drink of the nectar of life even when the contrast is great and the journey seems difficult or long. Help us to do that which seems impossible just as you do, and help us to create from a place of joy and a sense of timelessness.
Ho!

To the winds of the East - Hatun Kuntur, Great Condor, Apuchin, Huaman, Eagle, come to us from the place of the rising Sun, the place of our becoming.
Teach us to soar high and see those mountain tops we have only dared to dream of before, and help us to see with the eyes of the heart, to feel the guidance in our bodies, and to use our feelings as prayer.
Give us the broadest perspective and clearest vision of our most joyful and fulfilling destiny.
Take us under your wings and teach us to fly wing to wing with Great Spirit so that we create with self-effort and grace. Ho!

Pachamama, Santa Tierra Madre, Great Mother Earth.
We come here for the healing of all your children, beloved Mother.
Thank you for your breath and your waters, and the stone people,
the plant people, the two legged, the four legged, the creepy
crawlers, the finned, the furred, and the winged ones, all our
relations that are here not only to sustain us and bring us beauty
and joy, but to also teach us with their characteristics, their
instincts and their medicine that we can embody to help us along
the way.
Thank you for being our true Mother and for sustaining us with
your bounty, for supporting our healing work on your belly, and
for always taking those energies which are too heavy for us and
mulching them for us so that we don't have to carry them around
any longer, so that we can be truly free to create extraordinary
lives filled with joy, abundance, love, harmony, and support.
Ho!

Intitaita, Father Sun, Mamakia, Grandmother Moon, Hatun
Chaska, Star Nations, Star Brothers and Sisters, thank you for
rising everyday showering us with your light, your cycles, and
your love that makes life possible for us here, and for doing this
unconditionally without judgment, teaching us to treat ourselves in
the same way.
Hatun Apu Kuna, Great Holy Mountains, Great Lineage, and
Teachers of All times, thank you for helping us; and Ilaticha
Wirakocha, Wakantanka, Great Spirit, Creator, God, Creator of all-
that-is, you who are known by a thousands names and you who are
the unnamable One that dwells within us and all around us in all
forms, thank you for bringing us together to sing the song of life
one more day, to dance this dance of co-creation, and to take

Creation beyond where it has been before to new levels of joy, abundance, and exhilaration. Thank you for holding us.
Ho!

Make this prayer your own by changing it and feeling it in the moment. I never say it the same way twice and often do it silently concentrating more on the feeling. And you will have your own teams of non-physical helpers to acknowledge. It is always nice to open sacred space before an important act and to close the space afterward by releasing and thanking each helper in a similar fashion. Now that we have opened sacred space, we are ready to dream the world into being.

Chapter 2
The Deeper Secrets of the Mythic

The Powerful Influence of Myths

Humans and all the rest of Creation are continually participating in the expansion of Creation itself with the apparent help of some benign and unconditionally supportive Source. Another way to state it is that the very Source of Creation, the one consciousness or one spirit, appears to have differentiated itself into all physical and non-physical forms in the Universe from visible light to stardust, to radio waves, to atoms, to molecules, to single celled organisms, to multi-system organisms, to entire planets, to essentially all-that-is. And every single extension of that Source from stones to humans is expanding Creation for the fun of creating and interacting with increasing complexity and diversity.

As I mentioned earlier, according to Western mythology, on the seventh day of the creation of the world God rested, and all that was left was the naming of things. Creation is finished, it's over – closed. On the other hand, according to the mythology of the primary cultures as described by their medicine people, the people of power and knowledge, on the seventh day Great Spirit said, "I've created this much, now you finish it."

Up until the advent of Quantum Physics, Western Science had confined itself pretty much to the table of Western mythology. For example, the scientists have said that on the seventh nanosecond after the Big Bang, all of physics and the physical laws were created and all that was left was the naming of them – they essentially agreed with the religious mythologies without realizing it. And although they allowed for evolution, it was only an evolution of what already existed and not an adding onto Creation.

Quantum physicists have recently begun to understand and record the fact that the process of creation is still happening and we participate in it. They are just now catching up to the knowledge held for tens of thousands of years by the world's indigenous people. Now these physicists are even gathering evidence of and measuring an omnipresent and intelligent force or consciousness that has been around since the Big Bang or before, a force that Stephen Hawking goes so far as to call the "Mind of God." In fact, the Big Bang Theory itself has recently been refuted because of discoveries that matter is being created by black holes and that the Universe expansion is accelerating when it should be decelerating according to the theory.

A few great Western scientists, philosophers, thinkers, and seekers have been employing what Ken Wilber calls the *broad scientific method*. The scientific method itself consists of the following steps: 1) Injunction, which is to go do something like look into a microscope or solve a mathematical equation. 2) Observation and collection of data like "yes I see that skin is made of cells, or the square root of four equals two." 3) Corroboration with a statistically valid number of people doing the same thing and observing the same data. 4) Proof. By applying the four steps of the scientific method beyond just physically measurable phenomena we have the *broad scientific method*, which can be applied to prove well in advance that which even the finest of technological instruments may never be able to register. Westerners are simply used to the scientific method only being applied narrowly to the physical world. For example, even though cells are too small to see with the naked eye, the injunction would be to have a statistically valid number of people look through a microscope at a slice of tissue, like skin. Each would then share that they see a number of similar little units that link together to form the tissue, thus corroborating their observations, and voila, you have proof that cells exist. As an example of the broad scientific method being applied to non-physical phenomena (other than mathematics), the injunction may be to meditate three hours per day for one year and take note of your observations. Perhaps you had a vision of the Source, of God, or the Oneness of all that is. Then you check with a statistically valid number of people who did the exact same meditation. Each of them reports that they had the same vision of the Source (maybe you all saw a white light or burning bush that spoke to you, for example); thus, corroborating the experience and allowing you to claim proof that the Source exists and still speaks to us. Even though we cannot see it with the naked eye or hear it with our naked ears or through the aid of existing physical instrumentation.

Every scientific discovery can be said to be a leap from an old myth to a new myth. And sometimes these leaps require that a person of power step up and propose the new myth to begin with. Such audaciousness is the mark of a true leader, someone who can be a positive influence for change as opposed to being influenced by what is. A good characterization of this is a quote from Alberto in the introduction to a documentary titled "2012: The Odyssey" referring to the possible changes spoken of in the prophecies that reads:

> "We no longer live in the modern world, we live in the post-modern world. The structures of the

modern world which are founded on greed, on ever increasing economies, on ever increasing growth, on readily renewable resources.

That world has ended and does not exist anymore. We're living in a world of sustainability, of deep ecology, of great reverence for the Earth. If you haven't caught on yet that this is the world we are living in, you will probably be mulched."

How Myths Become True

So if it is true that Creation is still open and expanding, why does the Universe seem as static as if it was finished on the seventh day or seventh nanosecond? The answer could be because most of what we are creating is the same as what is already here. In other words, while everything is always changing or being created anew, it's just changing into the same thing or being recreated into the same thing. Most people are under this powerful influence of the current realities.

This occurs because by and large we are unaware of the process of creation and our role in it. For example, it is becoming more widely accepted that our thoughts create. Books like "Think and Grow Rich," movies like "The Secret," and practices like the power of positive thinking and creative visualization are just a few examples. Deepak Chopra conducted a study that shows that humans think on average 60,000 thoughts per day; and 95% of them are the same thoughts we thought yesterday. So if thoughts create reality, it is no wonder that our reality doesn't seem to change much

By observing and focusing on the current reality, we perpetuate it. And this isn't entirely a bad thing. A certain amount of stability is desirable as is the apparent buffer of time that we get between what we are asking to create and the manifestation of it. But it hasn't worked to our advantage to either shun the responsibility of our power to manifest, or remain completely unaware of how to properly play this game of creation. Shamans suggest that as we come into our power and freedom, as Creators, our ability to focus our thought and feeling energy on a preferred reality grows exponentially. Thus, it is to our great benefit and increased joy to learn how to harness this ability in order to use it in the most beneficial way possible.

A New Myth for a New Destiny
I offer this book as a method and a vision, with the intent of revealing the fun in the creative process that each of us is engaged in. This book offers a way to learn how to create the world we want more effectively. It also offers one possible vision that simply by the act of people reading it and expanding on it will make creating the world we want more probable – what I as a shaman would call a world destiny retrieval.

It is also important to note that creating the world we want or changing the destiny of the world must start with a full appreciation of the current reality. This is a bit of a paradox to most people since we have been mostly taught that in order to be motivated to change things, we have to be unhappy with the way they are now. Unfortunately, it is that very belief that makes it nearly impossible to change anything. The reason for this is that when we are in that state of unhappiness we are clearly focusing on "the problem" that we do not want, and that problem then dominates our signal, our asking, and the new signal is obscured. Whereas, if we can get ourselves to a neutral or happier appreciation even in the face of "the problem", then we allow "the solution" to manifest by allowing that signal to dominate. We must be in a state of appreciation for what *is* and be eager for what is coming next. We create not based on fear, discomfort, or disgust, but for the sheer fun of creating. So I offer this new vision of the world because I think it will be fun creating it in this way with you, knowing that the world is perfect just as it is now.

The New Myth Makers and Creators – "We are the ones that we have been waiting for"

Throughout known history there have been and still are groups of "elders" or visionary medicine people from sophisticated cultures such as the Hopi, Lakota, Maya, Inka, African, Australian, Tibetan, Celtic, and many others. These wise elders actively "dream" the world into being for the rest of us and for all life everywhere. Their dreaming as I described earlier is a ritualized visioning and feeling process—an active form of prayer, meditation, and mythic ceremony that deliberately and consciously engages with the Source of all-that-is to keep us and the world in beauty and in the Garden; or in many cases to bring it back there. And while one person deliberately creating in this way is more powerful than a million creating unconsciously, they have had their work cut out for them. Now is the time that we take some of the responsibility from their shoulders and step into our own power and freedom to choose the world that we wish to experience. It won't take many, just a critical mass of visionaries like you and me to bring about more of this so-called Heaven on Earth. Let this book be the drafting table of the new conscious creators, the next evolution of the Human species here on Earth.

70

In order to assist you in the process of dreaming the world into being through this book, a blank page where you can add your own vision and/or reshape or enhance my vision follows each section. Know that the words only serve to produce a mental vision and a bodily emotion; and the bodily emotion contains the most power of manifestation. And know that you can enhance the power by engaging the Mythic with ritual. This is why music, chanting, images, and mantras are also widely used with prayer, because of their powerful ability to bring forth emotion. I encourage you to use the pages in a way that gets you into the feeling place of the vision either with words and/or pictures, or just contemplating the blank page and stepping into that destiny with all of your senses using the power of your imagination. And use whatever tools, such as chanting or music, ceremony or ritual, that help you, and that you enjoy most. You can create a collage, Mandala, or alter to access the Mythic Layer. I find in creating that powerful bodily emotion, it helps to ask the question "How would it feel to be there now?" I also like the following technique to help you differentiate between a thought, a physical act, and a bodily emotion. Simply smile without moving your lips. Where do you *feel* the smile?

Chapter 3
How Does it All Work? - An Answer to the Universe and the Rules and Layers of the Game of Life

The Purpose, Basis, and Result of Life

Let's start with the simplest idea and work up in complexity from there. I am going to start by telling you the answer to the Universe. In *The Hitchhiker's Guide to the Galaxy*, the crew of a spaceship asks their all-knowing computer what the answer to the Universe is, and the computer emphatically tries to avoid giving the answer because it says they won't like it. Similarly, I offer the caveat that you may not like this part. It may seem too simple at first, but I assure you that it can be applied without fail to all situations, applications, and theories of Creation, no matter how complex they may become. Gravity is a very straightforward and simple law, but applying it in order to get a rocket to the moon can make it seem very complex.

So here it is, the answer is 42... told you that you wouldn't like it. No, that was the computer's answer; my answer is joy, fun, feeling good. And we experience that joy through the diverse and contrasting experiences and drama that this multi-faceted creation has to offer. I like to use the analogy of a theater. We don't go to a movie to see a bunch of people sitting around in bliss and perfect unity consciousness; we go for the drama, the ups and downs, and the pleasure and pain. And we usually don't just go to one movie; we keep going back for more. Of course, ideally our experiences are more pleasure than pain. And, just like in the theater where we keep it a secret from ourselves that we are just watching a screenplay with a bunch of actors and a director, so that we can be caught up in the drama, in life we purposely forget that all of our experiences are only our script. But if the pain becomes too great, just as we would do in the theater, we can ideally remember in that moment who we really are and that we are just living a script that can be rewritten. Regardless of whether we are considering all of the mechanisms and literal manifestations of our daily lives or some kind of multi-universal galactic re-unification or transcendence, from the most mundane to the most esoteric the line of questioning is simply "And why that?" or "What next?" And all such inquiries eventually lead to the answer "for the joy of it" or "because it feels good."

The question that follows this realization is why we don't consciously remember this secret from the day we are born. From the example of life as theater in the paragraph above, the answer is that life is not as much fun if you remember everything all of the time. It would be like knowing who will win the football game before it starts. Or constantly reminding yourself that the movie you are watching is just actors, a director and a script, instead of enjoying the exhilaration of being caught up in all the desires, thoughts, and emotions that the drama elicits. It is useful though to be able to remember, when the drama in our own lives has become too heavy or deeply troubling. Remembering this helps us to avoid spiraling down into a suicidal depression, or blowing the whole thing up and having to start over from the "Big Bang." Many religions, spiritual traditions, and practices are designed to get us to that place where we can remember and even reunite with the One as their final goal for our lives. Whereas Shamanism continues on to say that once you know how to remember and to find that unity with the One, what some call total Enlightenment, then the next step is to go ahead and forget again and come back to play in the theater. Thus, there really is no end or goal of Creation, just ways to have even more fun playing with it in what seem to be ever increasingly complex and fulfilling scripts.

As a side note, there are many mechanisms and manifestations that have developed in our bodies and minds that are the result of completely forgetting this secret and getting caught up in the dramas of life for thousands of years. Sort of like a filter that begins to be clogged, or like a machine that loses some of its functionality due to wear or poor maintenance. Examples include extensively documented issues such as not using all of our DNA and brain capacity, or malfunctions in the nervous and endocrine systems, and a multitude of other physical and mental pathologies and disease. In conjunction with these problems, many people also experience a general feeling of being disconnected from the Source and/or the Earth. These manifestations can begin to look and act like causes as well, and to some degree these physical and emotional issues do create deeper wounds. But we will not go into the details of all of these mechanisms here in this book, as there is plenty of information out there on such mechanisms, manifestations, and symptoms of the human condition. Instead, we will engage our focus as close to the Energetic and Mythic source as possible to elicit solutions that are more direct.

So that's it: the whole purpose of life is Joy. A by-product, or the result of life, is growth, expansion, and learning. Life doesn't have to be a school, where you have to graduate and work your way up through the grades after much struggle and suffering. For those who insist on holding onto that hypothesis, I'd say, "Okay then, it's a school, but then the only thing you have to get good at in order to succeed is recess." When we are living on purpose and in our joy, we are in our natural state of unconditional love and compassion. This state of love is what the Q'ero call *munay ki*, which translates loosely as "I love you" or "Be as thou art." This is our natural state and from this state, all creation is made possible. Struggling to "attain" this state through practices, without first clearing away the fears and wounds that cover it, is an uphill battle that can last lifetimes.

The very basis of life is freedom. This includes freedom to choose – you can even choose bondage, pain, and suffering, or to hold onto the hypothesis that life is a school. The Universe gives you evidence to support whatever hypothesis you choose, so you will always be right. Thus, if you insist that you are not free, the Universe will make you right, and it may take you years or lifetimes to dig your way out of that one. It is not uncommon to find these "double-binding contracts" in people where the belief is "I'm damned if I do and damned if I don't."

Even what I'm laying out here is a hypothesis just like the notion of gravity. But if you learn to work with this hypothesis and use the scientific method to run some experiments, collect some data, and compare it with others who are running the same experiment, you will be able to work wonders in your life, where miracles become the norm. We will cover later how to become freer from all influences in order to choose more consciously and deliberately to create more of the experiences you want and less of the experiences that you don't want – your preferred reality.

The Basic Rules of the Game
So here is how it works, or rather, here is how you, I, and All-That-Is have set up this game or theater for our maximum enjoyment when perhaps we were all just one undifferentiated conscious

Source sitting in the great Void. Nobody knows for sure, but it seems as though the Source split up into All-That-Is, or the Universe, with its differentiated forms of conscious expression, in order to start creation rolling and make our experiences more and more interesting and mysterious. As I once heard someone say, "We are all God playing hide and seek with herself." With this initial impulse came all of the various laws of Newtonian Physics, Quantum Physics, and Metaphysics, many of which have yet to be discovered or understood completely by the Western mind.

As discussed earlier, the Universe (All-That-Is) is still growing in complexity and diversity and expanding physically and non-physically. I think this is because it keeps things interesting and offers increasing opportunities for Source to play. The one original consciousness that now lives within each of us and in all forms is still aware of the game it's playing. Moreover, there are multitudes of ways or techniques to tap into that part of ourselves that can temporarily remember if we want to. We'll talk more about those techniques later.

The real fun is in staying mostly unaware of that undifferentiated writer/director/witness part of ourselves, so that we can keep playing the game immersed in all of the drama. In our Shamanic training, we call this "keeping a secret, even from yourself." It is of course best to come to that secret after going through the healing processes that without which we would be bound to repeat the dramas and wounds of the past, leaving us easily influenced and powerless. But once you become a person of true freedom and power having come to full clarity, knowledge, wisdom, and realization of who we truly are in all of our oneness—by whatever means, teachings and methods you resonate with—it certainly is fun to jump back in and play.

Now this leads us to the basic Universal laws or rules that make it possible for Creation to continue like this. Creation is just like any game and has rules that allow everyone to enjoy it in a predictable and repeatable way. I refer to these rules as: Resonance, Receptivity, and Momentum. They have to do with how energy, time, and space interact to provide the experiences and apparent solidity of what we have come to call the reality of existence. By understanding these basic rules and how they serve, we can then create steps that help us to play the game in a most effective and enjoyable way.

The Rule of Resonance
The first rule is the Rule of Resonance, which is very similar to the concept of resonant frequencies studied in physics. This Rule of Resonance is the asking part of "ask and it is given." Resonance is how we are creating our experiences, whether consciously or not. Some people think we create just by our thoughts, words, or prayer, but it is much more than that. The energy waves of asking come from our thoughts and emotions, both conscious and unconscious, and from every part of our body, both physical and non-physical (soul, aura, astral body, luminous energy field, whichever language or metaphor you choose). Thus, asking comes not just from the brain. This is where many teachers talk about the alignment of mind, heart, and spirit. Basically, we are bio-chemical, electro-magnetic extensions of Source energy constantly focusing and transmitting waves of energy based on our preferences and desires, or that of our influencers.

These asking waves of energy can be referred to as vibrations or frequencies, similar to those used when describing electromagnetic phenomenon such as light and radio waves. Asking waves can source themselves from memories of the past, observations of the present, or imaginations of the future; but regardless of their source, the Universe recognizes them as just energy waves. In turn, the Universe delivers in some form or another the experiences that match these asking waves of energy. Or another way to say it is that your experience of some event will match the waves of energy coming from you, whether you are conscious of emitting them or not.

People are often confused when they work hard to speak the words of what is desired, only to get something different in their experience. For example, you can say the words "I want to be healthy. I am healthy, healthy, healthy." But you could be actually sending out the vibration that matches "I am sick," if that is where your true focus of attention is. In this scenario, the Universe will deliver more sickness because this is the true vibration of the asking waves of energy. It takes some practice and internal awareness, as well as awareness and analysis of what you are receiving in your experience, to recognize and fine tune what you are really asking for relative to what you really desire. And it is very helpful to remember that you are asking for an experience, and not necessarily a particular object or event that brings you that experience. For example, I may want the experience of warmth and comfort under my feet and not necessarily need to buy a carpet for that to happen. Perhaps someone else gives me a carpet, or the experience comes from radiant heating or a pair of slippers.

Another important quality of the Rule of Resonance that may be the single biggest source of confusion for people is that the Universe is inclusive by nature, as opposed to exclusive. What this means is that the words and thoughts that attempt to exclude a particular experience have no effect on the asking signal. These words include: no, not, without, less, no more, stop, and so on. When I sit down with clients and ask what they want in their life, it is astonishing how many times I am told what they don't want. For example they will say, "I don't want this back pain anymore," instead of saying, "I want comfort in my body"; or, they will say, "I want to stop fighting with everyone around me," instead of saying, "I want harmonious relationships." Somehow, we have been trained to describe what we want in terms of what we don't want. Unless we are at an ice-cream shop where we tell the clerk the one or two flavors we want instead of listing the other thirty that we don't want. The bottom line is that if I pray for or ask, "I don't want to be sick anymore," the Universe only "hears" and responds to the vibration of sick, and brings me more of that experience. This is just like a two-year old child because they just recently came from the Universe. If you say to the child "Don't pick up that bottle," they will immediately grab the bottle. Have you heard the expression "The terrible twos?" It takes another year or two to understand that when we are told not to do something, it really means that our parents want us to do something else. The Universe never "learns" this and instead just keeps on answering our dominant signal. Try to see how those around you, and you yourself, respond to the question of "What do you want?"

A good analogy to describe this rule and the associated process of asking is that of a radio. When you want to experience certain music, which is really just a form of energy waves, say coming in on frequency 96.5 FM, you have to tune your radio to a frequency of 96.5 FM, a perfect match. When the signal in your radio is a perfect match to the signal carrying the music you prefer, it is selected from a floating mix of your radio signal and all other signals, and the preferred signal becomes amplified enough to come out clearly on your speakers and into your ears. This is because two matching frequencies will double in amplitude (strength) when they come in contact with each other. If you tune the radio to a frequency of 101 FM, then you cannot possibly experience what is on 96.5 FM; and, you will get what is on 101 FM whether you like it or not. The body-mind-soul, called you, is just like a radio. You have to tune your frequency to be a match to what you want to experience – because matching frequencies seem to attract and amplify one another. Since whatever frequency you are emitting matches with and amplifies the frequency of some experience that is out there just waiting to be called into focus, you in effect called on that experience.

You deliberately "tune your radio" by immersing yourself in the thought and emotional feeling of already having the desire manifested in your experience. I'll tell you the story of my first attempt at manifesting rain as an example. For a couple of years I had been learning and practicing organic farming. My wife and I had manifested living on a beautiful piece of land up in the foothills just north of Coyote, California. The land had abundant spring water and a feeling of sacredness from the Native Americans that had once lived there. Golden Eagles nested on the land, and wildlife was abundant. The owner had cleared a plateau that was about 80 by 40 feet and had a tremendous view of the rich valley below as well as the hills across the way extending as far as the eye could see. It was an ideal location for a substantial vegetable garden, and five years worth of horse manure was piled within walking distance, which was ideal for fertilizing the soil.

For my first couple of years of planting, I was able to grow beautiful crops of corn, squash, peppers, tomatoes, broccoli, and so on - enough to share with several of our neighbors for most of the year. By the third year, I was beginning to have trouble with the squirrels and deer, despite a colossal fence building effort. In fact, it was around that time that the neighbor's adolescent bull broke through the fence and destroyed my scarecrow. I thought a cow had gotten into the garden and went in to play with it. The playful "cow" started getting rough pretty quickly and I found myself perched on top of fence post until my dog successfully distracted the cow-turned-bull long enough for me to escape. It actually wasn't until then that I had noticed the smashed scarecrow and began to put two and two together – and yes, I confirmed my suspicions by looking more carefully at the hind side of the animal. I wasn't raised on a farm.

Suffice it to say that my interest in farming was beginning to wane. So as I planted the last of my corn seeds across the entire field and made my initial attempts for that year at getting the crop started, I realized that I wasn't going to have the time and energy that I had the previous years to really tend the garden. I needed nature to take over for me, so I decided to try this newly learned technique to call on rain. It was a sunny and warm early summer day, and the grass and sage on the surrounding hills had already turned brown. I stood in the middle of the garden and closed my eyes, imagining the feel of rain on my skin, the smell of it in the air, my feet in the mud, and my corn seeds germinating in the wet soil. I imagined the feeling of joy the rain brings to me so that my corn can grow and help feed my neighbors. I did this for a few minutes. Then I detached myself from the outcome by thinking "Oh well, if it doesn't rain, no big deal, I just won't have a garden this time around," and then I left the garden and walked back down the hill to our trailer.

For the rest of the day and the next morning I did whatever I could to distract myself from the garden and the weather so that I wasn't noticing that it was still sunny and not yet raining. If I did notice, then I would be asking for more sun and undoing my rain prayer. Lo and behold, later that day some clouds came through and rained on our hillside. I turned on the news, and the weather person mentioned this odd little bit of rain that showed up on the south valley. Since that rain, I have witnessed physical and verifiable phenomena over and over again that support the Rule of Resonance and the power of knowing how to apply it.

The Rule of Resonance, which is also referred to commonly as "The Law of Attraction" as introduced by Abraham-Hicks, is very useful for this game of life, just like the law of gravity is useful for getting around physically on this planet. Many books have been written on this subject alone. It is not necessary for anyone to understand how this rule works in order to live his life, just as it is not necessary to understand how a car works, or the rules of the road, in order to drive around. But if you want to fully enjoy your driving experience under all conditions and mostly stay out of trouble, or take it to a level of high-performance racing, then it becomes very helpful to understand as much as possible and know how to apply it effectively and deliberately. Similarly, it is helpful to understand the Rule of Resonance more fully if you wish to utilize it to get the maximum amount of joy in your life.

So we are always asking and it is always being given, whether what we are asking for is something we want to experience or don't want to experience. It is important to note that the Universe is responding to the core experience that we are really asking for, which can result in many different and mysterious physical manifestations. For example, I was asking for rain because I wanted the corn in my garden to grow, or so I thought. But the real desires, underneath the physical mechanism of having it rain so the corn would grow, were to experience my relationship with the Earth and the miracle of how she provides for us, to share this with my neighbors, to contribute to my community, and to feel the satisfaction and fulfillment of it all. The Universe could have come up with multitudes of other physical manifestations besides the rain and corn, in order to give me those same experiences with equal satisfaction and fulfillment.

In other words, the Universe knows what we really want, what we are really asking for at the core of our being, and orchestrates it in a way that fulfills the asking of every other living being so that the rule has no exceptions. This also means that sometimes your real asking, and the mechanisms that you think will achieve it, turn out to be a just part of the entire manifested experience. So the idea is to keep asking for all that you desire, but remain open to the details so as not to create resistance that ultimately may block the reception of what is being given. You may look back in your life and remember times when you noticed strange coincidences or synchronicities that were obvious, but also you may remember how you've received things you were asking for in less obvious and direct ways.

I'll give you another story to illustrate this "path of least resistance." Early in my Shamanic practice, I shared with my wife the ultimate fantasy for my work. I told her that I would love to be the shaman of a small village where I would get to sit in my hut all day and people would come in with questions and healing requests, and I would help then and just be fed and clothed and given a place to live and transportation for doing what I loved. And it would be ideal if it were in a setting similar to the Esalen Institute in Big Sur. At the time I shared this story we were living in San Jose and I was doing massage work in Santa Cruz, a good two hours north of Big Sur. I surrendered to the fact that there was no village like I had imagined anywhere near us, and even if there were, it would be unlikely to welcome a suburban kid calling himself a shaman. So that was the end of my fantasy, and I basically forgot all about it and just carried on doing what I was doing and finding ways to enjoy it.

After a period of time, a particular person started coming to the spa where I was working and became a regular client. We never engaged in much conversation, just focusing on the massage work. About a year passed by, and one day I mentioned to my client that I do shaman work as well and it may be helpful for an old injury that was still causing some issues. My client was open to the shaman session, and I explained that I had to come to their house since it was a private practice for me, which the spa that I was working in didn't care to offer, and, I didn't have a separate office at the time. It turned out that my client lived in Big Sur, so I planned the session into a nice little overnight trip with my wife.

As we approached the property where the client's house was, we were curious about the understated entrance and signs to this place called the Post Ranch Inn. The property was beautiful and it overlooked the ocean below and the entire coastline north and south. As I began setting up for the session, my client filled me in on the Post Ranch Inn - a small hotel and spa considered one of the best in the world. The Inn was built around the concept of returning to nature and renewing relationships (very Shamanic). It consists of the highest quality of service, and its architecture was designed to have the least possible amount of impact on the nature within and around the Inn. I was impressed by the whole concept and had never known that the place even existed.

My client enjoyed the shaman session in this magnificent setting, and before I left, suggested we go meet with the hotel's Spa Director. I was thinking she must be interested in a session as well; but to my surprise, she explained that they had wanted to offer Shamanism as part of their spa services for some time and wondered if I would be interested. I had to think about for a minute since it required that I give up half of my private practice, which at the time involved traveling to Miami once a month to work with a group of psychologists on some of their more difficult cases with amazing and rewarding results. It also meant moving off the property we had enjoyed so much and relocating to Monterey, a town in between Big Sur and San Jose, where my wife was working as a nurse. Then I remembered what I had asked for some time earlier. Here I was being offered the position of Shaman in Big Sur in a setting almost identical to the Esalen Institute, and what turned out to be a five star village! I gladly accepted the offer and began conducting shaman sessions in the yurt for the temporary villagers that come from all over the world to connect with nature and heal. And I marvel daily at how the Universe finds mysterious and clever ways to bring us the experiences that we are asking for from the core of our being.

The Rule of Receptivity

The second rule has to do with a buffer of time and is what we will call the Rule of Receptivity, or perhaps more accurately the "Art of Receptivity." This rule is also known through the teachings of Abraham-Hicks as the "Art of Allowing." Once you've managed to tune your frequency to match an experience that you desire by choosing the thoughts and getting into the feeling place of already having that experience, the next step is allowing the Universe to provide your desired experience. You may wonder why it doesn't happen instantly like with the radio. Why does it often take a while to get the experience you desire? And when you think that you are a match, why does it sometimes happen that you don't get exactly what you desire? It turns out that the real fun is more in playing the game than getting to an endpoint anyway. And while the endpoint is very satisfying for a time, we quickly become eager for the next game, the next desire, so we can keep playing. So for that reason and because of the fact that we are not experts at tuning our frequency to just the experience we desire, we have designed in a buffer of time that lets us change our frequency, or fine-tune it, to avoid disaster and to prolong the game.

Think of it this way, you would be devastated to hear music you can't stand at full blast, but you're not exactly sure where you need to tune the dial on your radio to get the music you want to hear. What the buffer of time allows us to do is try a station and as we begin to hear something we don't want, we can change the station

86

before it comes in full blast. The same thing is true in life, we aren't always sure what frequency we are emitting and in fact what experience we really want, so much of the time our experiences are a little off. And if we're still not sure what we want, the unwanted experiences will continue to intensify until we are a sure enough or motivated enough to change our frequency.

When we are not getting the experience that we want in any aspect of life, whether it is in our health or our relationships, I refer to that as contrast. And that contrast that we manifest helps us to become clear both about what we do want and about what frequencies we have been emitting. Instant manifestation of an experience would only be nice if we were already masters of tuning our frequencies (but, of course, then it would get boring again); we were brilliant in setting it up this way. For example, imagine if you had the frightful and unsolicited thought of a herd of elephants running through your living room. That is truly when the buffer of time comes in handy.

In fact, that reminds me of Drunvalo Melchizedek's description in his book, "The Ancient Secret of the Flower of Life," of a chamber located beneath one of the Egyptian pyramids that was used as part of the training program in one of their ancient mystery schools. Because of the specific and precise geometries and structures used to build the pyramid and chambers, as you move deeper into this particular chamber the buffer of time for manifestation shortens eventually to zero. As an initiate in the Ancient Egyptian mystery schools, you had to first go through 24 years of intense training and practice to eliminate all fears and learn how to control your thoughts before you could enter the chamber. When modern archeologists first uncovered and entered it, several died from snake and spider bites—from snakes and spiders that don't exist in Egypt! A few others suffocated from the fear of a lack of air in the chamber. That chamber is now barred and pad-locked for obvious safety concerns. Melchizedek himself gained special permission to enter and had a profound visionary experience; but it required all that he could muster to control his thoughts and not go to a place of fear.

Hand in hand with the buffer of time, the Rule or Art of Receptivity means that as long as you continue to match the frequency of the experience you want, it is on its way—you are basically in a receptive mode. As soon as you tune to another frequency that is not a match, you are blocking the experience from happening and, as Abraham would put it, the Universe is holding for you in "vibrational escrow." If you can manage at least to remain neutral relative to that frequency, the experience will still make its way to you, albeit somewhat weakened since your matching frequency isn't quite there. The buffer of time between asking and manifestation seems to correlate directly with your ability to stay in the receptive mode. And again, this is where many of the different spiritual practices can be helpful to you.

What I teach my clients and students is that if you find that focusing on the subject of your desire creates a feeling of resistance, there are two solutions. The first is to try to choose thoughts on the subject that feel better, and what usually works well is to get less detailed and more general. For example, the subject might be finding a compatible and enjoyable life partner. Until now you may have had a few attempts that didn't work out well, and now you've met someone that you think is the one but they don't seem as interested in you or are already with someone else. At first, you try to vision and manifest your life with this particular person, but you can feel the resistance related to their situation. That resistance is a result of the underlying vibration in you that is saying this person is not available. So instead of sticking to the thoughts that this particular person is the one for me and that "I and the Universe must make him my life partner," you may want to back off and choose thoughts like: "It is nice to know that there is at least one person so far that has the qualities I am looking for in a partner, and chances are there are more, and I am probably very close to meeting them. In fact, they may be even more perfect for me than this one, and wouldn't it be nice if they felt the same way about me and were totally available for me. I don't know exactly who they are yet, but I'll know it when they show up. What I really look forward to is the compatibility, fun, and pleasure of having at least one person in my life that I can count on to be with me for a long time, maybe even my whole life."

The second solution is to drop that particular subject altogether if you cannot find thoughts that have no feeling of resistance to them. Instead, find a subject that allows you to feel good in the moment. When you feel good in the moment, all that you have been asking for on all other subjects is allowed to come into your experience. So basically the most important thing is that you find excuses to feel good in each and every moment regardless of you current set of experiences. The thing that complicates all of this is that unlike a radio, we are not restricted to one frequency and one experience at a time. In fact, we are limitless in what we can tune to and experience all at once. We can even emit conflicting frequencies at the same time; we can use words or say one thing, but our whole being is emitting the opposite. So there can be much to keep track of and a lot of tuning of our frequencies around many subjects in our lives that we are experiencing and want to experience in perhaps a different way.

This is why we have offered ourselves so many techniques, philosophies, religions, and practices that focus on simplifying our lives and our desires until we master the game a little better. So it takes practice, and the good news is that we have an eternity. The problem is that some of us have forgotten the real reason why we have the practices in the first place, and instead, have made the practices the goal and purpose of life instead of simply joy. It's sort of like starting out in a Volkswagen Beetle to practice driving before you get in a Ferrari, but then becoming so attached to the Beetle, or convinced it's all you deserve, that you forget about the fun you would have driving a Ferrari. In fact, some may have tried to convince you of eternal suffering in hell if you even look at the Ferrari - more on that later.

Ask and It is Given – How Do I Receive It? And What Exactly Will It Look Like?

The Universe is benign and unconditionally supportive – ask and it is given, whether you want it or not and whether you have consciously asked for it or not. Whatever frequency your dominant thoughts and emotions are emitting, the Universe provides the matching frequency, and before long the experience is yours. The Universe does not judge, discriminate, or try to protect you, it simply objectively responds to frequencies. Therein lies your freedom, the very basis of your life. Remember we set it up this way when you and I were the Universe, all of it, the *one verse*.

So you are always asking with your frequencies, and you are always receiving/experiencing a perfect vibrational match, whether it is pleasant or not. The physical actions that we engage in are obviously an important part of creating our experiences as well, but if we align our thoughts and emotions before taking action, then our actions become inspired from a place of joy instead of assertive from a place of fear. The resulting action is then far more productive, effective, and hopefully fun.

Nobody can create your experiences for you. However, they can influence you consciously or unconsciously. The effect of this influence depends on how much you are in your power, meaning how deliberate and conscious you are at knowing what you are asking for and whether or not you are maintaining a match to it by how you feel in the moment. Later we will talk about how events of the past can influence you as well, but first we will discuss how those around you and your perceptions of the current reality influence you.

Someone once asked the Dalai Lama what the most important thing in the world is. Most thought he would say compassion or love, but instead his reply was "It's who you hang around with." He understands the power of influence in the creation of your reality. This is why one of the core practices in Shamanic training is not colluding with the consensus: not allowing yourself to fall under the influences of the people, events, planets, statistics, or evidence around you in the moment.

"I Couldn't Possibly Have Asked for That!"
People often ask how these rules apply to events like hurricanes, tsunamis, acts of violence, childhood death, abuse, genocide,

disease and so on. I often hear "Surely, those people are victims." Though it may take much more in-depth and lengthy study to fully understand, I shall offer some explanation here in order to clarify.

First, it is not necessarily a particular event or manifestation that is being asked for, but instead it is the *experience* of it. So a hurricane can be the answer to a collective of dominant frequencies asking for change, a challenge, a wakeup call, a cleansing, or to be noticed and given help, or just from a consistent fear of and focusing on the potentiality of the event. Each of these frequencies can be satisfied with experiences resulting from the apparent devastation of a hurricane or other large natural event. It is interesting to note that a person could also be in the path of a hurricane, but emerge unscathed, thus having a different experience than his neighbor. So the same event can produce as many different experiences as there are people involved in it, and it often does. This is why it is so valuable to pay attention to how we may be projecting our expected personal experience onto another, thus expecting them to have the same experience as we do, and finding fault in them if they do not. It always allows for more freedom and harmony in our own experience, if we reduce the tendency to project.

What about a child born with a deformity or disease? This could be the manifestation of a soul asking to come forth as a powerful teacher or inspiration, or to add to the diversity of life. It could also be the result of an unconscious pattern or imprint that is repeated through lifetimes or passed down from ancestors, and is therefore an unconscious asking coming from the wounded soul. The disease, illness, lack of balance, or major event is just the mechanism by which an asking is being fulfilled, not the particular thing that was asked for consciously or unconsciously.

In the case of the victim and perpetrator of an act of violence, it is often said that the perpetrator is actually in greater pain or fear than the victim. Again, this type of manifestation can be the result of repeated imprints, underlying fears, or catalysts for a greater healing. Likewise, when we see someone else going through an event, we tend to project onto him or her how we would experience it. We assume that that person feels how we would feel in the same situation, which may truly be much different from his or her own actual experience. Thus, we are compelled to play the third part of the victim, perpetrator, and rescuer trap.

From a broad, long-term perspective, what seems to be wrong, ill fated, unfair, or devastating, could actually turn out to be a blessing in disguise for the person or people having the experience. It may even preclude an even larger event, or greater contrasting experience, from occurring down the road. These types of experiences are certainly what we call contrast, which ultimately leads to strong new desires, or at least act as a sign post showing us an opportunity to heal the past, and to step into greater power and freedom. That great Universal Ochestrator that fulfills the "given" part seems to be infinitely complex and exponentially more capable relative to what we can understand with our human brains; which again reminds us that our judgment is futile and non-serving.

Momentum

Another important and related concept that we need to cover is momentum. There are a couple of ways to overcome the momentum of what your dominant frequency/asking has been creating in your experience. First, let us understand what momentum means and how it relates to our efforts to create the experience that we desire. Because of the buffer of time and the fact that we are equipped to be observational beings, the reality that we have been creating seems to remain stable over time. Remember the Deepak Chopra study that we discussed earlier, observing that the average human thinks over 60,000 thoughts a day (60,000 emanations of various frequencies), and that 95% of them are the exact same thoughts as the day before. Therefore, although our reality is changing constantly, it changes mostly into the same thing it was the moment before. One of the reasons that we continue to think the same thing is because we observe the reality as we perceive it to be, and then claim this perception as evidence to continue to hold the same habits of thought (which are also known as beliefs).

Another way to look at momentum is that all prophecy is self-fulfilling. Likewise, all diagnoses—whether literal, like from an M.D., or Psycho-spiritual, like from a psychologist or from a psychic—tend to add to the momentum. Momentum is what causes our past to spill over into our present and future. It is the difference between fate and destiny. What my teacher Alberto refers to as the Momentum Tunnel consists of narrow boundaries that have been dictated by our past and our subsequent expectations of the future, our own fated prophecy. The walls of that tunnel project into the future and dictate the most probable future experiences. It takes an act of power to shift the momentum tunnel such that other possible future experiences can become most probable, thus we choose our destined prophecy.

One night, my wife and I sat down with a group of friends and a well-known psychic, healer, and channeler who had spent years living with the Native Americans, and was once married to a Lakota Chief. This woman had tremendous psychic ability and a huge heart dedicated to service. When she first entered my friend's house with her assistant, she was very soft-spoken and even shy. We sat in a small circle and the woman started singing a Lakota song in her gentle feminine voice. After a few minutes, she began to channel an old Native American Chief, and her voice became decidedly masculine and the energy of the song thundered into the room and came to a crescendo that made the hair stand up on the back of my neck. The gentle woman was no longer present; we were sitting in front of a stern and warrior-like chief with completely masculine mannerisms and voice quality. We all asked a few questions to gain insight as to what our future looked like.

She/he could see that I was just beginning my formal shaman training, and accurately described many other details of all of our lives. She was reading our momentum tunnels. When she came to my wife, she said that she saw us adopting a Russian boy, and that he had been waiting for us and we should move quickly on the process. We were surprised, but also moved and inspired by her vision. Under what Greg Braden calls "The seduction of spirit." At the same time, we recognized that adopting a child was a huge step and commitment with many ramifications. When the channeling was over, we said our goodbyes and returned home with a sense of both excitement and awe. We quickly began to look into the adoption process and started setting our intent and engaging in our manifestation techniques, pre-paving the way for this destiny. We scoured international adoption websites looking at the pictures of the many-orphaned children, trying to get a sense of which one was waiting for us. It was overwhelming and confusing. In the back of our minds, we began to question just who had chosen this destiny; was it the child, the chief, the psychic, or us. We even contacted the psychic again, in order to gather more information to help focus our search.

The more we looked into the process, the more it seemed daunting, expensive, and complicated. Completely overwhelmed, we decided to put the process on hold in spite of the urgency of the reading. After a couple of weeks, I went to my first shaman class with Alberto, which happened to be titled "Reading the Signs of Destiny," and there I asked his advice about the adoption. He told me that now that I had started this training, the momentum of my life could radically change; and, in two months, the psychic might get an entirely different reading. He advised putting off the process until I had gone through some of the Shamanic training, which is essentially focused on our own healing and stepping into power and freedom, becoming completely unfettered from the influences of the past lives, ancestors, and current life traumas – the momentum tunnel.

Some months later and well into the Shamanic training process, we contacted the same psychic for a phone reading, and sure enough, this whole story of adoption was no longer part of the vision. My wife and I took our power and our destiny back, and know that the choice is always ours to make. And as shamans, we take special care in making sure that we do not add momentum to what we "see" in another's energy field, thus creating a self-fulfilling prophecy for them based on their old story. Instead, we stay out of the story and help the client map out their preferred destiny on the Energetic and Mythic layers.

Owing to the universal nature of these powerful concepts, we can employ the tools of science and mathematics as well to understand momentum. The mathematical equation for the momentum (p) of an object in motion is $p = mv$, which means that momentum is the product of an object's mass (m) multiplied by its velocity (v). The mathematical equation for the energy (E) required to change momentum is, $E = (mv^2)/2$, where m = the physical mass of the object, and v = the velocity or the speed at which the mass is traveling (distance / time). So, if we look at momentum (p) as the probability that our future experience will look just like our current experience—whether related to our health, relationships, career, or abundance—then the mass (m) would represent a specific aspect of our current experience, such as a disease, a marriage, our job or project, or the size of our bank account. The velocity (v) would represent our thoughts about our experience; where the frequency of a vibratory thought signal that we are emanating is given in cycles per second.

Now, we can apply our energy to change the momentum of an experience by changing the mass through surgery, divorce, a new job, new location, and so on, but such attempts at the Literal, or physical, level only changes the momentum on a one-to-one basis. Further, although taking these actions means that the specific aspect of our manifest reality has been changed, the underlying experience will tend to repeat itself, in one form or another, due to the underlying Energetic and Mythic pattern. Therefore, the tumor will appear in a different part of the body, or the new spouse or new job will bring up the same old issues as the previous spouse and job. These changes made at the Literal or physical levels are typically more disruptive and sometimes even traumatic than changes initiated at the Energetic and Mythic levels.

However, if we change the velocity, this reduces the energy required to change the momentum exponentially. This is because the velocity is squared (v^2) in the above formula, so any change to velocity has a very profound effect on energy. You can more effectively reduce the current momentum by bringing the velocity towards zero, or basically slowing down. If you get to time = infinity, then the velocity (distance divided by time) goes to zero, the energy and momentum equations go immediately to zero, and your experience is allowed to change gracefully with the least amount of effort. Meditation can help to reduce thoughts (distance) and Shamanic work helps increase the time. In fact, shamans refer to their work as stepping outside of time into infinity.

The Energetic intent of this book goes beyond the encouragement to change our habits of thought, and goes directly into a taste of timeless infinity. This is why we started with the opening of sacred space; this book itself creates a *huaca*, a quantum tunnel outside of ordinary time and space where the veil between the physical and non-physical worlds becomes thin, and therefore the time between the dream and the manifestations becomes shorter. This is the elegant way to dream a new destiny into existence.

Alberto uses a great analogy to describe the process of changing from a destiny based on the momentum of the past, which is just fate, to a destiny that we consciously choose and prefer. He says it's like you're in a truck racing down a long straight road at 70

MPH loaded up with the bathtub, refrigerator, sink, and all of your possessions, which can represent your job, your partner, your house, your health. And all of a sudden you decide you don't like where the truck is heading and you want to make a change; you want to choose and live a new destiny, so you grip the wheel and jerk it to the left without slowing the truck down. What is likely to happen is that most of the stuff in the back of the truck will keep going straight and be jettisoned, and there is a good chance the truck will veer out of control, roll, and cause a lot of damage. In other words, you'll lose the house, the marriage, the job, and go through a significant crisis, filled with pain and trauma. The other option, which is the Shamanic way, would be to slow the truck down or stop it completely; perhaps first gently and gracefully removing an item or two that doesn't serve or doesn't desire to join you on the new path. Then make the turn with ease and elegance, and accelerate on the road to your new destiny.

The Four Layers of Life Experience
Shamans see all of life experience to be composed of four layers or domains that we visualize as a series of nested eggs. We refer to these layers as the Literal, Psycho-spiritual, Mythic, and Essential. The language of the Literal layer is atoms and molecules. The language of the Psycho-spiritual layer is words. The language of the Mythic layer is images, ceremony, and ritual. The language of the Essential layer is pure energy. In the Western culture, we generally only recognize and work with the outer two layers. However, we will see how much more effective it is to work with all four layers, particularly in healing and manifesting.

These four layers have been written about and discussed from
many perspectives, modalities, and philosophical approaches. We
have heard of body, mind, and spirit, or of the manifest, conscious,
subconscious, and ethereal. Modern Psychology has come closest
to the Mythic with various forms of Deep, Integral, and
Transpersonal Psychologies as well as Jung's archetypes of the
Collective Unconscious. The main difference between Jung's
approach and the Shamanic perspective is that Jung considered the
archetypes and collective unconscious to be elements of the
psyche, whereas shamans see them as extra-psychic forces existing
in all of the natural Universe.

The Literal
The outermost Literal layer is what we in the West call the
consensus reality. It is the sum of all of all of our experiences; it's
our health, our bodies, our relationships, our work, and our
physical environment. This is the leading edge of creation,
the physical extensions of Source energy. In their practicality, the
shamans recognize this as equally important to all other aspects of
creation. This view contrasts that of many religious and
spiritual paths that make transcendence of this layer, and all of its
contrasting experience, the goal—and the way to bliss or Heaven.
The major conflict in the Western mind and world can be traced to
our love for and continued attempted mastery of the Literal with
our sciences and consumerism, which is in stark contrast with the
Western religious view our view that all of this materialism is
somehow evil or at least devoid of spirit. Whereas, the "beauty
way" of the native cultures of the Americas is a celebration of the
Literal world that is one and the same as Great Spirit; where there
is no separation of spirit and matter and where unity consciousness
is reflected in how they speak. For example, a Native American

would add the words "in me" to every object – that tree in me, that mountain in me, that bird in me, that person in me.

The allopathic Western medicines diagnose and intervene primarily at this Literal layer, the *somatic*. Nonetheless, in the West there is growing support for, and evidence of, the notion that the Literal layer is informed, organized, or created by the next layer, the Psycho-spiritual. This new body of research is being referred to as Psychosomatic Medicine and is well established in the Shamanic approach.

The Psycho-spiritual
The Psycho-spiritual layer consists of our thoughts and all that are related to them: the desires, emotions, beliefs, and perceptions – the focus of our dominant frequencies of asking as previously described. Most well known Western and Eastern healing modalities and spiritual practices focus primarily on changing the outer two layers: the Literal and the Psycho-spiritual, or body and mind. Whether through physical, chemical, mental, or Energetic intervention, these modalities attempt to intervene at and alter one or both of the Literal or Psycho-spiritual levels to bring about change in our lives; and they can be very effective—at least temporarily. It should be noted that any approach to healing can also affect the Mythic and Essential layers under certain circumstances or over a period of time, but it comes down which approach, or combination of approaches, will get you there most quickly, easily, effectively, and efficiently.

The Mythic
The Mythic layer contains the cultural, familial, religious, social, and personal mythologies or stories that operate mostly below the

radar of our conscious awareness. We even carry some of these with us from lifetime to lifetime and from generation to generation, as they are a part of our soul. Simply put, these are the "you should, and you shouldn't, you can and you can't, you are and you aren't" and they determine our concepts of who we are, where we are from, and where we are going. They are the maps of our epic journeys. For example, if you are a parent, you should behave in this way, and you shouldn't do that. If you are a woman, you should do this, and you can't do that, or in our society and religion, you must do this, and you must not do that. They shape our soul's journey and are ultimately old myths and stories that may no longer serve us and need to be shed, while new myths that do serve us would need to be created. In fact, the shamans say that much of the Western mythology has worn itself out and no longer applies to the new humans.

The myths are like maps or storyboards of epic journeys. They are often depicted and engaged through images, archetypes, fairy tale stories, and symbolic rituals and ceremony. They are generally difficult to describe in words, as they mostly live in our subconscious. An important distinction to make is that the Mythic I am referring to is not only the definition we are used to thinking of in terms of that which has no basis in reality, or fictional stories. The myths and the Mythic that I refer to from my Shamanic perspective can have their basis in real and verifiable stories as well as those that may have been imagined.

To illustrate the power of the Mythic layer in shaping our lives, I shall bring to light some of the most influential stories in Western culture that come from the Old Testament of the King James version of the Bible and the Torah. For example, in Genesis

God banished us from the Garden of Eden. But we are the only ones that were kicked out of the Garden; the Inka, the Hopi, the Lakota, the Maya, the Hindu, the Buddhist, the sub-Saharan Africans, and Australian Aborigines in their original stories were all left to be stewards of the Garden. And, not only were we banished; but we were kicked out for eating the fruit of the tree of knowledge and power. Most indigenous cultures go on vision quests to obtain power and knowledge, including Jesus' 40 days and nights in the desert, and Siddhartha's meditation under the Bodhi tree.

Moreover, not only were we punished for tasting this power and knowledge, but it was the woman's fault, for Eve tempted Adam with the apple. Further, ours is the only mythology where the masculine gives birth to the feminine (Eve comes from Adam's rib). So if you put just those first few pages of our most influential Mythic stories together, you can see how the Western cultures have developed an antagonistic relationship with the feminine, the very Mother Earth that sustains us and forms our bodies, all of nature and women in general, and where Westerners have been taught to believe that spirit does not dwell. Matter (Latin: mater = mother) has become inanimate, without spirit. Instead, all that is good and that is our salvation comes from the Father in Heaven. As a result, the feminine in both men and woman has lost its value and nurturing qualities. It's only "by the sweat of our brow" that we can gain our sustenance from the Earth, which mostly produces "thorns and thistles." As I've heard my teacher Alberto jokingly say, check this out the next time you stay in a motel, in case you do not have a Bible at home. This has become our primary experience in the West regardless of whether or not you were

103

raised in a religion, or have worked on changing your beliefs about it on the Psycho-spiritual level.

So now is the time to go back to the Garden and taste the other fruit, and to get back our rightful power, freedom, and knowledge as Creators. It was only because of our Western mythologies that we mistakenly believed that we had lost it in the first place. The Western mythology is a mythology and subsequent psychology of redemption; one in which we no longer believed that we even had the power to heal ourselves, and to take ourselves back to the Garden to taste of the fruit of the tree of everlasting life and become as gods. Instead, we were told that we must seek approval and redemption from some powerful judge who rules over us and is separate from us; or, that only through loyalty to a particular savior or church could we be allowed back into the Garden, or into the Heaven of our Father. The shamans say that we never really left the Garden, and true enlightenment, power, freedom, and joy are just a matter of remembering this fact. And that, instead of seeking to redeem ourselves, we can regain our power and knowledge by simply shedding these myths that keep us in a state of helpless woundedness and fear, and by re-shaping our beliefs in ways that keep us from uncovering or evolving into a higher consciousness and creating more of the Heaven that already exists on Earth. This Shamanic view is an example of creating a new mythology; and the shamans also recognize the great souls who have come forth throughout history to help us remember our true nature with their simple messages.

Another result of our Western mythology is that we have overvalued the masculine and logic-oriented mind, locking ourselves into the mode of hunters and gatherers of information by observation. Moreover, we have essentially made it a sin to follow our ultimate guidance system, which consists of feeling anything good in our bodies/heart and gut/intuition - the feminine. Through the Shamanic healing process, we can bring back the value of our bodies/feelings/feminine and use our observations in balance with our remembered abilities to envision and feel our new reality into being. We remember to know by how we feel in our gut, whether we are aligned with, and therefore allowing, our preferred reality to manifest. In this way, information becomes knowledge. The shamans say that information is being able to state that "water is H_2O," whereas knowledge is being able to make it rain.

In the Shamanic work of the West, where old mythologies are shed, we explore and bring to consciousness those ancestral and past life myths so that we can honor them, acknowledge their gifts, and then free ourselves from their binds on us. This is the true purpose of Shamanic ancestor altars. We make sure by the Mythic action of creating and tending to an altar, that we have honored, thanked, forgiven, and acknowledged the gifts of our ancestors, while making sure that they (and their mythologies) stay on the altar and no longer follow us around. When the Q'ero first saw Alberto and his students walk into their hut, they told him that Westerners don't know how to bury our dead. Alberto asked what they meant, since clearly we have funerals, crematoriums, and cemeteries. And their reply was that when Alberto and his students came into the room, the Q'ero could see the spirits of the party's ancestors walking in right behind them. In the end, disconnecting from the ancestors allows both parties to be free and to evolve into greater freedom, power, and joy.

My mother's side of the family had a powerful myth that I believe had been largely responsible for my grandmother and mother's cancers, as well as my own sickly childhood. This myth was most powerfully traceable to my great grandfather, Vincent Gecan. From his picture taken in the early 1900's, I could see that he was optimistic and generous. If you look at pictures taken before 1930, it is rare to find anyone smiling, and usually their grooming and demeanor appear impeccable. In his picture, my great-grandfather, who must have been in his mid-forties at the time, had a great big warm smile and somewhat unkempt hair.

This is his story as passed on by one of his sons:

> Vincent Gecan was born on April 5, 1862 in Propudnik, Croatia (which was formerly under Austrian rule, and after World War I, became a part of the new country, Yugoslavia). At about age fourteen he went to sea, as was common at that time. His first voyage was to South America, and subsequently, he made a number of such sailings, including to the United States. He married Ursula Stiglich in Croatia in 1886 or 1887. They had 17 children, 10 of whom survived to adulthood. He built a large home for his family in Croatia. Within a few years, they moved to Chicago as he had friends there and manual labor was in demand.
>
> Vincent was employed as foreman by a streetcar company called Chicago Surface Lines. Streetcar lines were being extended to the outer edges of the city, usually before the streets were paved. His crew was working on extending Lawrence Avenue tracks, and was finishing work on the

installation of the crossing of the Chicago, Milwaukee and St. Paul train tracks. It was there, while he reviewed programs, progress and requirements, that a car pulled up to the crossing. The conductor got off the car, as required, walked to the center of the tracks, and gave the signal for the motorman to proceed across the tracks. This was standard procedure. When the streetcar pulled onto the track, the motorman saw a train bearing down. He panicked, grabbed the power control, opened the door, and ran down the road. The conductor did the same. Vincent saw the impending crash, got on the car, ordered all the people to get off the front end of the car, but he was still on the back platform when the train hit. He and another man were killed instantly. Seven of his crewmembers were injured from flying debris, and one other was killed. This fatal accident occurred at 10:35 A.M. Monday, Jan. 24, 1916, which was also his youngest child's 6th birthday.

The fact that Vincent responded in the manner he did was no surprise to those who knew him. The story aroused the interest of all the newspapers in Chicago, which all proclaimed Vincent a hero. Vincent had saved lives before. In 1896, he jumped from the North St. Bridge over the north fork of the Chicago River to save a 4-year-old boy who had fallen through the ties. He landed on an ice floe, breaking through it, but he managed to pull the boy to safety. In 1901, he also rescued a woman from a burning building. Vincent was perceived as a man of great strength, courage, & leadership. He was a man of justice and compassion, yet very sensitive, kind, and extremely helpful to his fellow man.

The legend of Vincent's generosity is a powerful one in my family. He would bring a gift for his children on his way home from work everyday, even if it were just a loaf of bread. My mother still keeps a copy of the newspaper with his story on the front.

This hero archetype is one of self-sacrifice, martyrdom, and optimistic stoicism. The gift is strength, courage, leadership, and good cheer in the face of adversity, and of course being of great service. But, when the threads of the Mythic hero are controlling you and your beliefs and you do not constantly have a life to save, the downfall is a lack of self-value and worthiness that often manifests in disease or as the wounded healer who has not yet healed. For my grandmother and mother, it meant the constant stress of worry and sacrifices that never fully allowed them to live their own passions and desires but always dictated they appear cheerful and happy regardless, so as not to trouble anyone else. The manifestations ultimately showed up as physical disease, namely several types of cancer. In others, I have seen this type of sacrifice lead to feelings of resentment as well.

The tricky thing is that society so greatly loves and admires the hero archetype that it is difficult to shed. Personally, I was following the same track, holding the same beliefs on all levels of my being. If I had continued this way, it may have led to the same toxic buildup and death that had stalked my grandmother and was stalking my mom. Through my own Shamanic healing journey, I have shed that hero myth, and it has healed my ancestors as well, even improving the health of my mother and allowing her to be more open about her own truth and desires. Now I am free to play the hero if I choose, but I am not compelled to do so in order to feel valuable to the world. That is a big difference.

I may find myself in a situation to save lives at the potential loss of my own—but at least I would be healthy, conscious, deliberate, and ready if the time comes in that way. Nevertheless, if that opportunity does not present itself for me in this lifetime, I will still feel valuable and worthy of being a human. Shedding this myth also allows me to be of service to the world as a shaman healer while maintaining my health, well-being, and joy. It is no longer necessary to follow the old story or myth of gaining healing powers through sacrifice. The new myth of the healthy, happy, abundant, and fully functioning healer not only serves me better, but allows me to be available for that much more work and to be of greater service to the world in the long run. The idea behind shedding myths is to have the benefits that our woundedness had been providing, but without paying the price. Ask yourself what myths you would rewrite that would allow you to be more fully alive and of even greater service, if that is where your joy lies.

The Mythic layer is engaged and changed in very powerful ceremonies such as the Navajo Medicine woman's sand painting, or similarly through a Tibetan Buddhist monk's Mandala. There is also an increasingly popular method of solving issues in business and psychology that is known as *Constellations*, or emergent role-playing. Constellations were introduced into modern culture by Bert Hellinger who was inspired by methods used in certain indigenous cultures in South Africa. You can also create your own powerful Mythic ceremonies. To illustrate, if you go to a Navajo Medicine woman for a healing, she will listen to your complaints and create a sand painting on the desert floor with many colors and details. At some point, this sand painting not only symbolizes your life, it actually becomes your life by tapping into the Mythic layer of your being. Then all she has to do is change the sand painting, and it will change your life. She can remove the genetic predisposition to heart disease, and that funky relationship, and replace them with a healthy heart and a healthy relationship. The Tibetan monks will create a similar type of Mandala on a street corner to restore balance to a city for example. This is also how a Haitian voodoo priest works with a doll, but we hear of them using these methods more often to harm than to heal. Another example is if I go to a Tarot Card reader, a tea leaf reader, or even an astrologer or psychic. They all often work primarily with the Mythic layer. They use archetypical symbols to see what you are likely calling into your experience or what you have called in the past and present. If the Tarot reader places the cards and finds that there is one that indicates I may loose everything soon, for example, what I will do as a shaman in an act of power and love is to remove that card and replace it with one whose meaning is something I would prefer to experience. This is similar to working with the sand painting. Creating an altar, or a collage works on the Mythic layer, and all of these ways of working with the Mythic layer belong to all of us.

The Essential

Just attempting to step beyond or re-write our mythologies is often not enough, for they are informed by the even broader reaching Essential Energetic layer – the blueprint or template for the rest of the layers. And it is through engaging our healing at the Energetic that we will ultimately be able to obtain the freedom and power to consciously dream a better world into being.

The Vedic teachings of India refer to the components of this layer as the Aura and Chakras. My shamans call it the Luminous Energy Field and Wheels of Light. Others call it the Light Body. And in the West, we know it as the Soul. It is like an electro-magnetic field in the shape of a toroid with conduits (the chakras) through which information is passed to and from the nervous system. The clearer the luminous body becomes, the more visible it becomes, and eventually it shines so bright that some painters depict it as a halo.

Throughout history, many people have pondered the mystery of the soul, the afterlife, and reincarnation. These people have contemplated the question of when the soul actually enters the body. It is actually more fluid and unpredictable than most imagine. I have seen full-grown adults whose souls have yet to fully enter their bodies, and I have seen souls so anxious to be born that they are already in their mother's body before the ovum is fertilized. I have also seen others that are taking advantage of someone who is not completely owning and fully occupying their body by coming along for the ride. And there is everything in between – just as diverse as the possibilities when we are fully incarnated. Human souls can even temporarily move outside of their physical bodies and travel through space and time without limits. They can also move in and out of objects, plants, or animals at will; the indigenous medicine people that are known as shapeshifters master this ability in order to gain useful information.

The concept of reincarnation is often misunderstood and therefore often dismissed. People wonder if they were an animal, a tree, or a stone in their previous lives, or whether they could be one of these forms in their next life. While I wouldn't completely rule out the possibility, it is more likely that once the highly differentiated soul of a human has a human experience, it is unlikely to become less differentiated like the stones, plants, or animals. This is because we are attracted to the possibility of new and more interesting dramas, just as movies have evolved from soundless black and white moving pictures to computer generated graphics with extraordinary special effects. It seems to me that, just like nature seeks more and more complexity, we seek more and more complex experiences, more opportunities for contrast, and therefore greater joy. But the Buddhist traditions believe that the goal is to get to the stage of development where the soul is capable of choosing to either re-merge with the One source or to re-incarnate in order to help others get to that stage. The shamans would call this the place of choosing a place of total freedom and power, but they further recognize that the soul may prefer a third choice of just diving back into the drama of life for the sole purpose of playing, as it may be even more enjoyable than permanent Nirvana. This gets back to the notion that without contrast, anything would become monotonous after a while. I've presented my own insight into the soul and how it relates to population increases and decreases in Appendix B.

Our Quantum Physicists are just now telling us about this essential Energetic layer that has always been the consensus reality of the primary cultures for millennia. Further, cosmologists now recognize that some 96% of the known Universe is made up of something they have not been able to measure or define directly through their scientific methods. They have labeled this mysterious aspect of the Universe "dark matter" or "dark energy." Quantum science is recognizing that everything is made up of energy, or light, at its core; and matter is just denser light (Latin:

chromo). And by measuring light and matter, they have recognized that energy often switches states between the two and can be affected by the observation and consciousness of the observer.

According to my teacher Alberto, this essential Energetic layer organizes the other three layers the same way a magnet organizes iron filings on a plate of glass above it. You can move the iron filings around all you want, but they will eventually re-align themselves to the magnetic field. Only when we change the magnetic field itself do we create lasting changes in how the iron filings are organized. When we become clean energetic slates, we have the ultimate freedom in choosing the frequencies that emanate from our Mythic stories and our Psycho-spiritual thoughts, later becoming our Literal reality. Having and using our creative power from that place of freedom and love is what ultimately serves us and serves all of creation.

So this eternal soup of Energetic waves is the source of the physical world - the matrix so to speak. It is the implicate order that becomes explicit in a form that matches the frequency and direction of our thoughts and emotions, like a hologram that can project different images depending on the frequency and angle of the light that is shined upon it. It is also holographic in that every single part of it contains the ability to project/manifest the entire explicit reality. And like with a hologram, it is somewhat illusory or ineffective to believe that just fiddling around with the explicit, the outermost layers, is going to create a permanent and lasting change. It may seem to do so in the short term, but the real and eternally lasting change must take place at the Essential source.

Taking the idea of the hologram one step further, there are Western scientific philosophies and much indigenous knowledge that describe what we experience as reality to be more of a personal choosing process than that of co-creation. This means that all possible realities already exist and that by aligning our thoughts and feelings we are simply choosing one of them, just like the hologram and the angled light. So as we engage in this process of focusing our attention, our vision, and our feelings/emotions within the sacred space of these pages and with the help of all life everywhere, we have our hands directly in the soup, and we are aligning our taste buds with the flavors we want most to experience. We are choosing what we want to eat at the buffet. We are changing the implicate order of the hologram, as well as the nature of the light and how we are shining it to create our explicit reality, the experiences we prefer.

In order to facilitate deep and lasting healing, the shamans focus less on the intervention or cure of the Literal and Psycho-spiritual layers, and more on the original source coming from the Mythic and Essential layers. And when they say lasting, they mean for many lifetimes and generations going forward and backward in time. For it is these two most "inner layers" that inform, organize, and create the two "outer layers" of the Psycho-spiritual and Literal experiences; with the Essential consisting of the core Energetic blueprint, or template, and the Mythic consisting of the map or instructions, the archetypical story of our life. Shamans have recognized that it is also easier to address an issue by engaging it on these inner layers before it manifests in the outer layers.

It is also true that with enough time and effort, it is possible to effect change on the Mythic and Essential layers by doing work just on the Literal and Psycho-spiritual, but from what I have experienced, this is like trying to empty a water tank with a spoon in the middle of a rainstorm, as opposed to just pulling the plug at the bottom of the tank and draining it all at once. Instead, the truly effective approach, which some call Integrative Medicine, would be to address all four layers of our being. To stick with the Latin vernacular, I would call it Chromo-Mythos-Psycho-Somatic medicine. Or I like to call it Applied Quantum Physics.

Now it is true that not all of our experiences are sourced from the Essential or Mythic layers, some things just happen on the Literal and/or Psycho-spiritual. For example, if you choose to stop eating, you will starve to death. And if you choose to run in front of a speeding train, your body will be severely and irreversibly damaged. And if you submit your psyche to enough traumas, it too may be severely and irreversibly damaged. This is how our original wounds came to be lodged in our Essential and Mythic layers in the first place if they were not completely processed in the moment of their happening. So new things can and do happen that have the potential to affect us on all four layers; but they do not have to. If we do ceremony, or are able to process and release these events in the moment, then they will not affect our Mythic and Essential layers.

This is where the core healing techniques of Shamanism come in. When we eat and process food, the heavy ash that we cannot process leaves the bottom of our body and is returned to the Earth, where it's mulched into fertilizer for new life. Similarly, when a traumatic or painful event occurs, ideally we are able to fully express our anger, grief, or fear and allow the heavy energies that we cannot process to leave the first chakra and enter the Earth, where it is processed and made available for new life. If we hold or block the release, then it builds up in our luminous body and chakras, dulling them and creating imprints that can later be triggered to repeat the same experience. The Shamanic healing techniques help us to release those old energies quickly and gently once and for all, like an Energetic enema. If you observe animals in the wild, they will show you how they release energies in the moment after a traumatic event. For example, a gazelle that narrowly escapes the grip of a hungry lion, upon achieving a safe distance will stop and allow its body to shiver from head to toe. This probably helps burn off any excess adrenaline from the cells, while also helping to release and send the heavy energies of the trauma to the Earth.

There is a significant amount of material and research available on the specific interactions of certain chakras and the physical body and mind, as well as correlations between imprints in the luminous energy field and disease. For example, I have found that people whose seventh, or crown, chakra is blocked tend to experience that they are not supported or provided for by a father figure and/or God, so they tend to feel that nothing will get done unless they do it themselves. Those with the first, or root, chakra blocked tend to experience not feeling supported by a mother figure or the Earth, so they do not feel nurtured and are unable to release their heavy emotions. And since it is our nature to project onto others, the ones with the blocked crown chakra must play father or God for everyone else, making their decisions for them and feeling they need to do everything for them. The ones with the blocked root chakra tend to play mother or Earth for everyone else, taking on all of their shit, and feeling compelled to play the role of the caretaker.

Occasionally I have clients with both the root and crown chakras blocked and they are often manic, completely exhausted or diagnosed with chronic fatigue syndrome, and overly engaged with people and events of the past, present, and future. These engagements appear as Energetic cords coming mostly from the third chakra at the solar plexus and are feeble and unsuccessful attempts to make up for the infinitely abundant cords that would normally be attached from the Source to the crown chakra, and to the Earth from the root chakra. Cutting the engagement cords and re-establishing the Source and Earth cords brings the person's level of energy and calmness back.

The other chakras have their basic psychosomatic associations as well. For example, the second chakra is related to anxiety and adrenal glands; the third to relationship issues and intestines; the fourth to self-judgment, love, lungs, heart, and liver; the fifth to knowing and speaking our truth, being supported, thyroid glands, and pancreas; and the sixth to the senses and to understanding and seeing the true nature of ourselves and the world around us. The luminous energy field is often affected by a spilling out of the built-up heavy energies of the chakras, or cords, and imprints connecting us to the Energetic patterns of our ancestors, as well as being affected by significant physical and emotional traumas that occur often in the same area of the body that the Energetic imprints are located.

Chapter 4
The Five Steps to Dreaming Your World into Being

I offer this five-step guide for the process of deliberately manifesting any experience into your reality. This can be used for anything from having more playtime, to preserving more rainforests, to creating world peace. Just remember that you cannot create an experience for somebody else, but if enough people are asking for the same experience, then it will be shared, and the influence can spread. Also remember that if this process is not working well for you, it is likely the result of unconscious beliefs, or Mythic and Energetic influences that are sabotaging your efforts. A quick trip to your local shaman for a session and some Mythic homework and belief work should help tremendously.

Step 1: Acknowledge and Bless the Contrast
Acknowledge those aspects of your current experience, "reality," that you do not want – the contrast – and decide what you do want – the preferred experience. Part of this acknowledgment is to be grateful for the clarity that the contrast has given you, and its overall enrichment of your life experience. This is where the great teachings of compassion, unconditioned love, and non-judgment are helpful, so that we do not get trapped in the role of the victim of this contrasting experience. Instead, we recognize our role in creating the contrast for our own benefit—and often the benefit of others, who have played a role in our contrast, or in whose contrast we have played a role.

Step 2: Appreciate what You Can about your Current Experience

Find all the aspects of your current experience that you can appreciate, and focus your attention on them. You will know that you are doing this well when you feel good. If you are not feeling good, then change whatever you are thinking about, looking at, listening to, acting on, or talking about in that moment until you find that thought, word, action or observation that feels better. It may take some time and effort to work your way from feeling really bad (like being angry), to feeling really good, (like being blissful), about any particular subject. However, each step of progression makes the next step more available. So pat yourself on the back if you go from enraged to frustrated, or from frustrated to pessimistic, because the next steps will take you from pessimistic to hopeful, then optimistic, then satisfied, then cheerful and so on. If you are having trouble working your way up the scale of feeling bad to feeling good on a particular subject, for example politics, then switch your attention to a completely different subject that you can more easily work up the scale with: for instance, relationships. This is helpful because as long as you are feeling better about any subject, you are allowing experiences regarding all other subjects to also improve for you.

Step 3: Find and Feel the Core of Your Desired Experience

Determine the core of what you really want, and start imagining what that experience will feel like. For example, with respect to your relationships, you may at first think you want a particular person to become your partner. But maybe the core of what you want is to experience unconditional love and support, pleasure, laughter, and security with someone that you find attractive. To the extent that you *can* be more specific about the "package" that

119

your experience will come in, without feeling any resistance, then go ahead and imagine how the specifics will look and feel. But if you begin to feel any resistance as you try to be specific, then it is essential to back off to a more general experience that feels good.

Step 4: Become Unattached to the Outcome

Release your attachment to receiving what you want. In other words, find the attitude that it is okay if you do not receive what you have asked for, so that you can keep your attention focused elsewhere. This is a paradox, but it allows your desired experience to manifest more quickly. The reason is that if you are noticing that what you have asked for has not arrived yet, you are essentially asking for the absence of it, and canceling out your original feeling-based request or prayer. The Universe takes time to orchestrate all of the synchronicities and events necessary to give you the experience you have asked for.

Step 5: Be Open to the Unexpected

The Universe always delivers the experience you have asked for, and it may be in a completely surprising or unexpected way or manifest form. In order to receive the experience that is waiting at your door, it is essential that you remain Energetically open to whatever package or mode of delivery it comes in. The best way to do that is by repeating step 2. And remember to go deep within your feelings, your body, and your heart with a sense of self-love, and therefore love for all that is, in order to determine the core of your desire and remain open to the wonder and beauty of this Universal gift. In the meantime, be accepting of all, and make the choices and take the actions that feel inspired.

Getting into a meditative or quiet state of mind and body can greatly increase the effectiveness of aligning your thoughts and emotions with your desired experience. You can accomplish this by rhythmic drumbeats or rattling, chanting, rhythmic movement, yoga, physical pleasure, or other methods of getting into a pleasant altered state of consciousness during or before this dreaming into being process. In Appendix A, I've listed several practical short-term meditation practices that my students and I have found helpful over the years.

Part 2
Applying the Shamanic Knowledge and Visionary Process to Dream the World Into Being

Vision for the World

As we step into this portion of the book, let me repeat what I said earlier: My viewpoints and vision may seem overly simplified; and that is okay because this isn't about solving all of the world's problems or getting rid of any of the contrast. We are not attempting to create some kind of panacea for every situation and every living creature. There will always be tremendous diversity, and it will continue to grow; but the important thing here is to know that you can deliberately and consciously choose the parts of the diversity that you would like to see grow in your experience and in our collective experience. Also know that much of this particular vision may already be taking place on various scales somewhere in the world, and if that is the case, this book serves to bring them into broader manifestation, as well.

Now that we know how and why it all works, let's focus on the specific details of this world, our creation, and make use of our power and knowledge to bring about the changes that may serve better. The following is my vision, my offering of frequencies through the words and ideas presented at the time of this writing. While it's not necessary that anyone else choose to offer these same frequencies for me to have the experience I'm asking for, the power of more people adding their frequencies helps the power of the vision become exponentially greater. Thus, a shared vision helps to bring about the experiences more quickly and more collectively. So as you read these pages, I encourage you to modify and tune the vision to your own desires, and to pay attention to how they make you feel. Because before the experience manifests, it is our ability to be aware of our feelings that lets us know if our current vision, or offering of frequency, is a match to what we really desire.

At the very least, I hope these pages encourage you to become more aware of your own true desires—and whether or not what you are thinking, saying, feeling, emoting, and observing (i.e. where you're setting your radio dial) is serving to manifest your desires into your experience. One of the surest ways to feel good, and to therefore be a match to your core desires, is to find appreciation for what is right now. Hence, the world is perfect and wonderful just the way it is. Now, let's see how we can choose an even better one. Each section that follows contains some background and explanation of the contrast in order to sharpen the vision.

Chapter 5
Health and Healthcare

I start with health because it is fundamental to everything else we intend to do, be, or have. We start with the notion that we are essentially non-physical souls temporarily focused in this physical time-space reality using our body-mind as a vehicle. With the help of our body-mind vehicle, we are able to focus our energy and use our feelings as our guidance, in order to create and enjoy our world. The extent of our ability to gather, store, and utilize energy through our vehicle, and to be aware of how we feel, determines the extent in both quantity and quality of our life experience. Anything that hampers that ability is non-serving, and anything that helps it is serving. The great shamans of the world see poor health, illness, disease, and low energy as an opportunity to rise to an even greater level of health than before. This is the same as the principle of contrast described earlier – through greater contrast, we become more clear and focused on the state of health that we really want.

This is a different way of approaching health than is widely accepted in Western cultures, where illness and disease is seen as a stroke of misfortune that gives us the opportunity only to return to where we started, and perhaps learn something in the process. The Western view is that poor health is something that stalks you, where the microbes and jaguars have you on their lunch menu, and if you are not careful then you will fall victim to them or to your faulty DNA for example. Approaching health from the victim/perpetrator/rescuer triangle is counter to how the Universe really works. According to the Rule of Resonance, there can be no victim or perpetrator, and therefore no need for a rescuer. But until we get to the point where this reality is more widely accepted, the current approaches to health are a necessary part of an integral, or holistic, healthcare system.

Currently, the Western approach to health is that of engaging in battle with a predatory world. This is tied in with our mythology and how we approach nearly all of the contrasting experiences in our lives. And this mythology needs to evolve as we ourselves evolve from the way of the violent victim warrior to the way of the peaceful creator warrior. For example, the current Western myth frames our medicine by talking about the "battle" against cancer or an "arsenal" of drugs. Thus, we even use the language of war and fighting. And like most wars, when the arsenal of weapons has been exhausted, like what is currently happening with antibiotics, the war is lost. In the case of antibiotics, we may even be hastening the both the end and the loss of the war. This is because the widespread use of antibiotics has sped up the evolution of more virulent, drug-resistant strains of bacteria. Some battles may be won in the short term, but the war is lost in the long run.

We will certainly benefit from a new approach, one in which we can focus our medicine on empowering our body's natural abilities to find harmony and balance with the world of microbes and toxins. This has served us for millennia, but modern Western medicine has inadvertently undone most of the benefits of Natural Selection and biological evolution just in the last fifty years. This is due in part to our expectation that more technology will make up for any damage we create, and ultimately save the day. Again, many aspects of modern medicine are a superband welcome adjunct to improving our quality of life; and, these beneficial aspects should continue to advance. However, we may want to reconsider the aspects that have created biological time bombs.

Another important distinction between the Western approach to health, and that of the shamans is that biologists say that genetic evolution only happens between generations, whereas the shamans say that it can happen within generations. This Shamanic view means that we are not helplessly tied to our DNA or the predispositions that we may have inherited from our mother and father. Instead, by engaging healing at the core Energetic blueprint, we can alter our DNA, which ultimately alters not only our bodies but also how we live and heal.

Many practitioners of traditional Western medicine, and even Alternative medicine, focus their education and approach on the mechanisms and manifestations of disease, often confusing the symptoms with the causes. For example, a "new age" practitioner may point to imbalances in the body's Chi, or the limited use of all available DNA, as the cause for some disease. This practitioner may then employ various methods to re-balance the Chi or re-activate the DNA. Likewise, a Western psychiatrist may point to a chemical imbalance in the brain as the cause for the disease. On the other hand, by focusing comprehensively on all levels of our being, the Shamanic approach addresses the true cause, and pays very little attention to any mechanisms and manifestations. This is because the manifestations, like a broken bone or chemical imbalance, are not the real source of the problem. Thus, the shaman may recognize that a part of the person's soul is missing, or that there is an energy or entity in their soul that does not belong. The shaman will then see to it that the unwelcome energy is removed and that the soul is restored to wholeness. The shaman recognizes that the condition of the soul or luminous energy field was the true cause for the imbalanced Chi, inactive DNA, and chemical imbalances that were manifesting into the particular disease. By addressing the source directly, the natural mechanisms for restoring balance are allowed to fully function once again.

Our Western medicine and many alternative medicines continue to seek technological approaches on the Literal level or Psycho-spiritual level to improve health; and with enough effort and intent, it is possible for these approaches to eventually affect the Mythic and Energetic layers. Thus, even the shamans do not have a monopoly on effecting change on all layers; they just tend to lead toward the quickest, simplest, and easiest way to do it. The ideal approach would be an integration of Western and Shamanic technology, because it could speed up the overall manifestation of the Energetic work, and buy us the time to heal more now.

The Western approach alone can also be invasive, cumbersome, and ultimately impermanent. It also has the potential for harmful side effects. This is true not only for internal medicine but also for mental healthcare and the exclusive use of psychology or psychiatry, as well as the many "new age" approaches. They seem a little messy, fragile, and time-consuming relative to the elegant and quick approach of working directly on the Energetic and Mythic layers with the ancient and modern Shamanic practices. When both the Shamanic and Western approaches are used together, the results are extraordinary.

For example, a significant part of my early private practice involved working closely with a group of psychologists and psychiatrists on their more difficult cases. For two years, I traveled cross-country once a month to work with them. One case in particular stands out for me. It involved a woman who was diagnosed with manic depression and paranoid schizophrenia, was suicidal, and had been in psychotherapy and on psychiatric medication for eight years. She was divorced, and only had visiting rights with her 10 year-old daughter. She was denied custody because of her condition, and her ex-husband, who was physically abusive, was given full custody. Despite spending numerous years in therapy with some of the top doctors in the country, which had given her Psycho-spiritual understanding of her entire life and condition, she could not stop herself from cutting her wrists and ending up in the hospital on a regular basis. When she first came into the office for our session, I could see the lifelessness in her on all levels. Death had already claimed her, though on the surface, she was a young, intelligent, successful, and attractive working mother.

She shared her story with me with an understandably defeatist attitude, even showing me the numerous scars on her wrists (there had to be at least thirty). As part of the intake interview, I helped her describe a vision of what she would like her life to look like if there were no limitations. Under most circumstances, this can be difficult for anyone to do who has not yet been healed. But this set a goal by which we could measure the results of the work, and helped me to start tracking where the blocks were in her luminous energy field. The process of clearing her energy field was fairly complex, and involved healing the deep past life wounding, soul loss, entities, and ancestral/Mythic threads. Typically each of these aspects are healed in separate sessions, but I was determined to do all that I could for her in that moment, as I wasn't certain if and when I would see her again.

It turned out that she had a natural ability to see energies very clearly, so she was able to describe all the forces of nature and non-physical healers that I work with in accurate detail. Never before had anyone been able to acknowledge this gift of hers. Normally, a first session would last about two hours including the explanation and intake interview, where the actual Energetic work takes typically one hour and can be much quicker. I try to accomplish as much as possible in a single session that serves the client, and therefore my sessions tend to be one-and-a-half to two hours. Her session lasted nearly four hours.

We cleared a tremendous amount of Energetic sludge and patterns that did not belong and did not serve her in achieving the preferred life that she had described. I performed the Death Rites, to clear the death that had been stalking and slowly claiming her. We also brought back the huge part of her soul that had been missing for lifetimes, because the world had not been safe for it to return due to a very traumatic event. Along with this soul part, we returned her passion for life, her gifts, and a power animal to help her keep the soul part safe from now on. All of this was done on the Energetic level.

Up until this healing, every one of her experiences in this lifetime had been more recent versions of the ancient wounds that had left imprints in her luminous energy field/soul and were manifesting over and over in slightly different forms. It was also complicated by the fact that an outside entity had taken up residence in her body, and was influencing her and causing the incongruent "voices" in her psyche. This turned out to be a beloved aunt, who had a history of mental illness and addictive behavior, who died suddenly and unconsciously and was therefore lost and confused, not fully realizing she had died, and not taking the opportunity to pass into the next world where she would have had the inherently broader non-physical perspective. When this happens, the departed souls often seeks comfort with the ones they love, and the ones whose energies seem bright and strong, which are often children that they were close to in the family. I helped the aunt to heal and understand that there was a better place for her to go where she would be greeted by loved ones, and also be free of the confusion and pain; and, that her niece would be better off being the sole inhabitant of her own body.

By the end of the session, my client was smiling and joking for the first time that she could remember. We mapped out some homework and tools for her so that she could integrate all of this work that we had done on the essential Energetic layer into the Mythic and Psycho-spiritual layers. A few days after the session, she went in for her weekly psychotherapy session, and it was clear to both her and the therapist that a major breakthrough had occurred. Life had reclaimed her. She took up her creative outlets of art and music once again. She felt valuable and worthy as a mother and fully functioning human being. She had desires and reasons to live and honor her own life and gifts. She recognized her beauty, and loved herself. Her relationship with her ex-husband even began to shift, and after a couple of follow-up sessions, he allowed her to have joint custody of her daughter. The symptoms and mechanisms of her diagnoses disappeared, although advisedly she maintained her regimen with her doctors.

These are the kind of results I've experienced in great numbers with the integral approach of working on all four layers. Another interesting case illustrates not only the importance of working on all four layers, but also the power of other peoples' influence over us when we are not in our power. A close friend, I will call Jim, had experienced my Shamanic work and had taken my class on Thetahealing, and through both had experienced powerful results. The Thetahealing technique is what I use to speed up the integration and manifestation of the Energetic and Mythic work into the Psycho-spiritual and Literal levels.

Thetahealing techniques work directly with the Source of all creation to instantly change whole belief systems, both conscious and unconscious, and make instant changes to the physical. Otherwise, it could take weeks to months for the work on the luminous energy body and myths, to become manifest in reality. In some cases, the momentum of the literal reality is too great to change in this lifetime regardless of the core healing that has taken place at the Energetic blueprint. In the Thetahealing technique, instead of channeling the healing energies through their own being, the healer calls on and witnesses the energies going direct from the Source into the client's being, thereby removing any limitations related to the healer's own stage of development. The process is very simple and easy to learn and apply by anyone, even on themselves, with miraculous results.

Jim's wife, who I will call Maria, was a strict Catholic and ran the weekly Bible study group at her church. She was very gifted in this regard, and well respected for her ability to clearly interpret and communicate the teachings of the Bible. While we enjoyed each other's company as friends, she was not interested in experiencing or even really discussing my work as a shaman. To her there was no other Godly way than the Bible, and I honored that. One day I received a very solemn call from Jim. He explained that Maria had been experiencing pain in her stomach area, and difficulty with her digestion for some time. When she finally visited a doctor about it, the CT scan showed a cancerous tumor in her stomach lining about the size of a baseball. She was scheduled for surgery to remove the tumor within about one week.

Maria was terrified of the prospect of being cut open with a knife. She was so terrified in fact, that she was even willing to have me work on her, but only with the Thetahealing techniques – no Shamanism. I met with her and Jim together three days before the scheduled surgery. I knew from experience that Thetahealing could dissolve tumors. Applying the Thetahealing techniques, for the first hour, I tested for and changed belief systems related to her beliefs on worthiness (of receiving and healing) and on instantaneous healing. Then I asked Jim to simply send up a prayer of unconditional love for Maria, while I moved my consciousness out of my body and up into Space above all the energetic influences of the planet, and commanded (manifest with) Source/God to dissolve the cancer cells. I then witnessed the energy of Source and Jim's unconditional love coming doing into Maria's body and doing the work in her stomach lining. I imagined her whole and healthy in every way.

After the healing session, I left Jim and Maria without any expectations for results, and particularly because I had not had the opportunity to clear the Energetic imprints and work on her mythological influences. It was a powerful session nonetheless, and Jim and Maria were both appreciative and hopeful. About four days later, I received a call from Jim, and I could hear the smile and awe in his voice. Before the scheduled surgery, following normal procedure, the doctor ran one more CT scan to confirm the size and location of the tumor, and it wasn't there. Jim said the doctor just stood there looking at the scan and shaking his head in disbelief. The doctor wanted to cut her open anyway just to be sure. But since Maria was feeling better, pain free, and able to eat well, they high-tailed it out of the hospital, and went directly on a previously scheduled vacation to Mexico for two weeks.

They had a great time in Mexico, and Maria's stomach felt better than ever; and, she could eat anything she wanted, digesting it with ease. Soon after their return home, Maria went into her Bible study group, and they were all very interested and concerned about her condition. She explained very cheerfully that she was feeling great, and that they had a wonderful vacation in Mexico. Their concern deepened as they asked, "What about the cancer, didn't you have the surgery?" Maria explained to them that a healer friend of Jim's came over three days before the scheduled surgery, and dissolved the tumor. At that point, their concern for her reached a fever pitch as they reminded her that only Jesus could heal, and that she had better go back to the doctor to make sure that there wasn't some mistake. The group's powerful beliefs dictated that it was impossible for anyone other than Jesus, or a Saint, to perform the miracle of an instant healing.

Their powerful influence on Maria in that moment, although well intentioned, activated the Energetic imprint, and re-established the old beliefs, because we had not cleared her essential Energetic and Mythic layers during the healing session, which would have brought her more fully into her power. Had she allowed me to do that part of the work, I'm convinced that regardless of the influence of her group and their beliefs, she would have maintained her vibration of well-being. Instead, she waited a couple of weeks while she struggled with the words of her friends and the influences of her past wounds and mythologies, and then finally went back to see the doctor for another CT scan. The tumor had reappeared, but in a different location in the stomach lining; and, by the time I talked with Jim again, she had already undergone the surgery, and we never talked about it again. All I could do is pray to one of my healing team members, Jesus, to continue to help Maria on her healing journey. For I understand that my Shamanic practice is not the only way, and in time, healing happens regardless of the approach.

By contrast, I had another client named Paola, for whom I had conducted a shaman session that helped her to regain her self-love and come into her power regarding the relationships with her family. She had two teenage daughters, one teenage son, a very commanding and opinionated husband, and an extended family that were helping to suppress her own desires. They all lived on the other side of the country from where I lived. The self-love that we had helped her to reclaim included loving her body as well as all other aspects of herself, even though she was somewhat concerned about her weight.

One day, my wife Gina and I were enjoying lunch together at a sunny outdoor restaurant next to the ocean near Santa Barbara, California. It was just a spontaneous little getaway for us. I got a call on my cell phone that turned out to be Paola. She had been recently diagnosed with uterine cancer that had progressed to the point that her doctor was recommending a hysterectomy, a complete removal of her uterus, which is an all too common procedure. She did not want the surgery, and asked me to do some Thetahealing for her to see if we could make a difference.

Since every part of my shaman work is equally effective over distances, or non-locally, I went to work the minute I hung up the phone. Gina was happy to help as the technique took only a couple of minutes. As we sat at the table, I had Gina send up unconditional love for Paola, and I commanded the energy of Source and the extra unconditional love to dissolve the cancer in Paola's uterus as I witnessed the work being done. Within days, test results confirmed that her Uterus was clear enough to keep in her body. Three years later and after doing sessions for her entire family, Paola was happier and healthier and more in her power than ever before, and enjoying all of her relationships.

The techniques and results that I have described are commonplace to the shamans of the world. I hear and see evidence of many similar and even more spectacular stories of miraculous healings from other shamans and energy medicine healers of all backgrounds and training. I've been asked on a number of occasions why these results are not all over the news and why resources and funding have not been directed towards in-depth mainstream research. I can only speculate and speak from my own experience that the mainstream institutions and health industries that would lend credibility to these alternative approaches are too entrenched in their paradigms and/or are mostly interested in researching approaches from a purely financial incentive. And since the techniques used in Shamanic work do not fall within the narrowly defined scientific paradigm of the mainstream institutions, I understand their skepticism and reluctance to commit resources towards further study of them.

The techniques that I have described can be done by anyone with the training and desire to heal themselves and to empower others to heal. A growth in the number of skilled Shamanic healers would likely undermine the relatively new, rapidly growing, and highly influential sixty billion dollar drug and healthcare industries. These industries attempt to marry elements of wanting to do the best thing to help people, while also trying to be as profitable as possible to further their and their investor's goals. It is messy as is usual for *Homo sapiens*. Nevertheless, attitudes and awareness are changing very rapidly and significant interest, acceptance, and research is being directed toward energy medicine as the results are becoming increasingly difficult to ignore or discount.

Though I have emphasized the importance of working on the essential and Mythic layers, it is equally important to work on the Psycho-spiritual and Literal layers. As much exposure as I get to the world of healers, psychics, and yogis, I've observed time and again that many people have engaged in work that has blown open their chakras, particularly the upper chakras, but have not done the necessary psychological work, or have become so detached from the Literal world that they have become dysfunctional. And in the extreme, some will end up in mental institutions, or at least heavily medicated. Numerous clients have come to me in various stages of psychological distress, and I'll sometimes end up referring them to a good psychotherapist, or just help them come back to the practicality and tools of everyday life in the physical. There is a Zen saying that goes "Before enlightenment, chop wood, carry water…after enlightenment, chop wood, carry water," for we cannot forget that we choose to be here in the physical. Therefore, a balance of work on all four layers is really the ultimate integral approach to healing and staying healthy as physical human beings.

There is one particular story that stands out as a very good illustration of this issue. The story starts with a journey my wife and I took to India, to visit the ashram of a renowned yogi named Sathya Sai Baba. Now Gina and I had had years of study with yogis and had spent time in ashrams here in the United States, so we were somewhat familiar with the interesting personalities, nuances, and traps that one can find in any group of seekers and in any spiritual institution. I was particularly interested in Sai Baba because of his ability to manifest objects out of thin air, among other amazing abilities. I had seen this on videos but really had to see it with my own eyes, still having a healthy skepticism. In addition, we wanted to take our favorite healer with us as a treat, since he had not been to India in years, and had done so much great work for us.

The three of us made the long journey to one of Sai Baba's ashrams near Bangalore in a town known as Brindhavin. India itself was so amazing, so full of contrast; I would characterize it as the heart of the Universe. It is all there, from extreme poverty and degradation, to extreme wealth and beauty, from the most advanced technology to a complete lack of technology, and so on all within the length of a city block. Thousands of people from all over the world came to live in the ashram and see Sai Baba speak everyday. Most came hoping that he would grant them a miracle, and/or that they would get a personal audience with him, which seemed to have the same odds of winning the lottery.

The first day was blazing hot and bone dry in the football-field-sized courtyard facing the stage where Sai Baba would make his entrance. Surrounding the courtyard were the multi-storied buildings that were mostly dormitories for the devotees along with two large cafeterias, one for the local Indians, and one for the Westerners. In order to arrange the seating in an orderly fashion, we all got into one of about twenty lines of probably one hundred people each. The wild monkeys already had their seats along the walls and eaves of the surrounding structures.

When a line was let into the main seating area, more often than not, the mild-mannered vegetarian students of yoga made a mad dash for the best opportunity to get near Sai Baba, as he would later stroll through the audience picking who he would see privately. We saw a few people get knocked over, usually by a middle-aged woman. What contrast compared to the quiet and serene ashrams we were used to! Sai Baba made his appearance and gave his talk for the day, then strolled through the audience taking letters, bestowing blessings, and manifesting ash and rice out of thin air. I did my best to see that it was not coming from his sleeve or some other sleight of hand. At one point he was within five feet of where we were sitting, close enough for me to see very clearly some grains of rice form a couple of inches below his hand in mid-air, just before he scooped them up and placed them in eagerly awaiting hands. This observation, along with an interesting visual effect that I noticed when I would close my eyes after looking at Sai Baba, together with an amazing experience that Gina had in answer to a request she had made (that

I discuss below), satisfied my skeptical curiosity. Of course, I might have been what Greg Braden calls "Under the seduction of spirit," and therefore seeing what I wanted to see; but nonetheless, it was satisfying.

Gina's experience on the other hand had a tremendous impact. She had simply asked to experience true bliss. That night she had a dream that she was chosen from a crowd by one of her beloved spiritual teachers known as Gurumayi. There was beautiful music playing, and Gina's greatest passion in life has always been dance. Gurumayi embraced Gina and began to dance with her. They began to spin, and at that moment, Gina experienced a feeling of pure joy like she had never known before. She awoke with the tears of joy running done her face, and the dream was so vivid, so tangible, her heart was still filled with that bliss. And to this day, she can remember that dream, and feel that bliss.

It seems that it was common for Sai Baba to see someone in private and tell him or her to stay at the ashram for longer than originally intended. My friend and healer who had come along with us, told us that one of the reasons for doing this was that Sai Baba recognized that the devotees in question, and the world in general, would be better off if these particular people stayed close to Sai Baba in the ashram. I was already convinced that I had seen enough and had learned what I wanted or needed to learn. So, I was going home as scheduled no matter what he might say to me.

On the last day, we were introduced to a group: a middle-aged German woman and four young adults from Sweden, along with a three-year-old boy and an infant that had been born to one of the young couples while they were at the ashram. They had formed a little group that appeared to be led by the German woman. One year earlier, during their planned one-week visit to the ashram, Sai Baba told the Swedes to stay longer, and he would let them know when it was time to go home. Shortly thereafter, the German woman, who had been at the ashram for seven years, took them under her wing.

I don't remember how we met them, but they needed money, so we gave them some, and they told us their story. One of the Swedish men had recently lost his newlywed wife, because she had refused to stay and went home as scheduled. This is where it gets interesting. The German woman claimed to have been completely purified and totally enlightened because of her years at the ashram. She claimed to have strong psychic abilities, and that in her dreams, Sai Baba regularly spoke to her and gave her instructions. When the young couple gave birth, apparently the German woman was psychically "told" that this was really her baby, and that he was the return of Jesus, and she was essentially mother Mary. She had the group convinced that they all had a mission together to bring this child to various churches all over the planet, including the Vatican to be blessed by the Pope in order to save the world.

Gina and I didn't know any of this while we were in India, we only found out later because we had told the group that if they ever needed a place to stay as they were passing through California, they could stay with us. Three months after our trip, we got a call at three a.m. on a Saturday morning saying that they were at the San Francisco airport, and could we come and get them. They ended up staying with us for a whole month little by little taking over our lives, until we finally realized what was going on, re-claimed our power and our house, and kicked them out.

When we thought back, we realized that there had been signs to alert us from the start. On the first day of their stay, the German woman told us that it was common for people to begin to question her intent, and to even begin to think of her as evil. And if that started to happen to us, it was just a test, and we should rest assured that she was completely pure and doing the work of God. The final tipping point for us came with a kind phone call from the German woman's ex-music partner, also a Sai Baba devotee and seemingly very rational, warning us of this woman's history of mental illness and subsequent manipulations.

The conclusion to be drawn from the story is two-fold, based upon both the woman and her followers. The first part is that no amount of Energetic purification alone guarantees your health as a fully functioning, sane human being. The second is that no amount of Energetic purification alone guarantees that you will become empowered enough to live your own life and to not be easily influenced by others. Thus, a balanced and comprehensive integral approach to healing on all four layers seems essential.

The integral approach to healing may look something like this: You've encountered a genetic condition, injury, or disease that is manifesting in your Literal and/or Psycho-spiritual experience, or you have prematurely entered the food chain of microbes, insects, or animals and your physical body has been compromised.

Step 1: Go to a Western doctor with the best technology and stop the bleeding, so to speak, in order to stay alive (buying you time) and come to some clarity of mind and body; this may mean surgery, drugs, and/or psychological crisis intervention.

Step 2: Go to an alternative healer that can increase the speed and efficiency of step 1; this could be any number of alternative healing approaches, ranging from Acupuncture and Herbs, to Reiki, Massage, Thetahealing, Shamanism, and so on.

Step 3: Now that the acute crisis is over, go to a shaman, begin the work of clearing the imprints and Energetic cords that attracted the imbalance and Literal manifestation in the first place, and learn and practice the techniques that will keep you balanced, and clear going forward.

Of course, if you do Steps 2 and 3 preventatively, you can likely avoid the Literal manifestation in the first place, or it will be minor enough not to need serious intervention. I like the following example that Alberto uses to describe the steps above. If a snake bites you, go to a doctor to stop the bleeding and remove the poison; then go to a shaman to figure out why you ran into the snake in the first place and why you couldn't get along with it. Then clear the death that is stalking you (lives within you) and learn to create the experience you would have preferred. This holds true whether it's a snakebite, mountain lion attack, hurricane, ex-husband, bird flu, or automobile accident.

So let us summarize what we can appreciate from the current contrast in health. The currently dominant approach to health based on modern Western culture has helped us to stay alive long enough to address the deeper causes of disease. It has also helped clarify and even scientifically prove, mostly through its limitations, that there is more going on than what we can observe on the physical and Psycho-spiritual levels, thus propelling our return to more holistic, deeper, and broader reaching approaches.

Vision for Health and Healthcare

My vision is that more health care professionals will begin to recognize the four levels of our being, and therefore allocate more resources towards helping clients come into their power and take a more creative and deliberate role in their own healing journeys. Shamans help in not only disinhibiting the body's natural healing systems, but also in teaching people how they can heal themselves on all levels with the power of creation and witnessing, with less focus on the diagnosis and treatment of symptoms and more focus on prevention and healing from the essential core of who we are. This means far more Shamanic energy medicine should be accepted, studied, and recognized as a primary approach to healing and prevention.

Treating the acute symptoms and situations with the Western approach and its technology will continue to be an important part of this integral medicine. However, it is much easier to engage and deal with a pending heart attack or cancer on the essential Energetic layer than in the ER. So this vision isn't just of preventative medicine like proper diet and exercise, but also it is a vision of working on all four levels and starting as far upstream and thereby as close to the true cause, as is possible. One great example of this is what my friend and colleague, Dean Taraborrelli, is doing in Sedona, Arizona around the treatment of addiction. His approach to rehab includes everything from the modern Western medical treatments to the Shamanic healing, and changes in diet and lifestyle.

The huge time and energy commitment in the education and practice will be required to play any one role in this integral vision, and it will require a team approach from experts in healing at every layer. My vision is of specialists from each layer (Literal and Psycho-spiritual Western medical doctors and Eastern and/or Alternative Medicine doctors, along with shamans that work in the Mythic and Energetic realms) work in full cooperation with each other and the client. These specialists will have a full appreciation of each other's gifts and strengths, working together toward the goals of not only greater health and self-empowerment for the client, but also of achieving the full potential of our species to experience the greatest joy.

Notes on Your Vision for Health and Healthcare:

Chapter 6
Relationships

Relationship is the fundamental mechanism of all creation. Some say that the one Source/Consciousness/God/Allah/Great Spirit/Atman/Creator emerged from the Void and decided to split into all the forms of the natural cosmos, both physical and non-physical, in order to experience itself. From monotonic Void to contrast and diversity—sounds exciting doesn't it. It seems to me that the Void would get boring after awhile, so I probably would have done the same thing. Would you? I think we did and still do!

Therefore, in order for Source to experience itself, we have this thing called relationship. Energies interacting, quarks relating to each other, atoms to each other, molecules, crystalline lattices, cells, organs, microbes, bugs, reptiles, fish, mammals, humans, organizations, countries, Heavenly bodies—and who knows where it really ends and where it begins, if at all. It is through relationship that we are able to enjoy dancing in and out of the expression and experience of our true nature of love and compassion.

Although many claim to know, we don't really know where creation starts and where it ends. Here we seem to be nonetheless. So the question is, what kind of relationships and experiences you as the human aspect of the Source would prefer. From the Shamanic perspective, there are five fundamental opportunities in, or reasons for, ideal relationships. The first is to provide unconditional support and appreciation/love for another, which requires a state of non-judging or allowing to obtain true intimacy. Second is to come together with a common vision/dream, which manifests exponentially more powerfully than the dream of a single person. Third is to provide pleasure, comfort, healing, joy, ecstatic union, and contrast on all levels. Fourth is to accomplish the physical aspects of creating through cooperative action. Fifth, sometimes referred to as shadow work, is to play a part in each other's scripts to show us the places where we can heal and come into our power.

The Inka shamans call the ideal relationship *ayni,* which also means reciprocity or harmony. When it comes to relationships, shamans are completely uncompromising, but totally negotiable. What this means is that there is never a need to give away your power and freedom, and never a need to compromise in what you choose to think/perceive and therefore experience. But, in order to get along so that our choices and experiences can harmoniously mesh with the choices of those we would like to continue to interact with in this fluid and time/space constrained reality, we need to be willing to negotiate. As just one example, let's say a husband and wife are figuring out how much time they can each spend with the kids relative to each other's responsibilities and interests, such as work and sports. A compromise would be that the wife keeps the job she hates and gives up the sport she loves, so that the husband can continue the job where he travels 60% of the time, and then go out on the boat to relax from the stress of the travel. Instead, the negotiation might involve each of them finding work they are passionate about, as well as fun activities they and the kids would enjoy doing together, while also setting aside some time alone to relax.

The Q'ero have a ceremony that they use to maintain *ayni* and the ability to continue to receive the gifts that the world has to offer them. This practice or ceremony is called an *ayni Despacho*. I find that many of my Western clients who have an abundance of material wealth and emotional support in their lives also have an underlying feeling that something is missing. As a result, they may even be unhappy and/or sabotage themselves by compromising what is truly important to them. Some attempt to fill this empty space with forms of charity, so that they feel as if they are giving something back of what they have received; but this does not always fulfill them. The ayni Despacho is the Q'ero's answer to this dilemma.

The actual ayni Despacho ceremony involves taking gift-wrapping paper and placing small portions or symbols of all the essential gifts they receive from the earth in their daily lives. For example, the Q'ero make offerings of grains and seeds, sugar and sweets, lama fat, aromatic herbs, animal crackers, cotton for the rain and clouds, a seashell for the ocean, representations of their house and tools, and so on. As they place the items on the paper, they give thanks and blow in the prayers with their breath. Additionally, they blow prayers of gratitude into a group of three leaves called a *kintu*, representing our three worlds, the conscious, the subconscious, and the superconscious, or in Quechua, the Kaypacha, the Ukupacha, and the Hanaqpacha. Often several *kintus* are used to release things that no longer serve, to express gratitude for all that they already have, and then as prayers of gratitude for what they have yet to receive. When the Despacho is complete and all wrapped up, one *kintu* is added for any forgotten prayers and then the bundle is wiped over the bodies of all those involved in order to cleanse away any of their remaining heavy energies into the Despacho as well. All of the energies, prayers, and offerings contained in the Despacho are then given to the earth by either burying it or burning it. Like with all forms of combustion or digestion, the useful energy and prayers are extracted, and the remaining ash is mulched into the earth to grow new life. The effort and intent that the ceremony requires takes care of that need to reciprocate, and therefore allows even more abundance in. Even outside of the ayni Despacho ceremony, the Q'ero are mindful of the value of symbolically returning a small portion of their gifts to the earth. For example, if you hand them a drink, they will dip their finger in and sprinkle some drops on the ground.

Another advantage that the shamans have in creating harmonious relationships is using the power of perception, which is based on the fundamental understanding that they create their own reality. My teacher Alberto describes it this way: in the west are people of the precept. We have Ten Commandments and books upon books of laws that dictate our relationships to just about everything in our lives. When we want to change our relationship to something, we write another law or precept about it. On the other hand, the shamans are people of the percept—when they want to change their relationship to something, they change their perception of it. They have no need for rules and laws in order to live in harmony and abundance for all. The Greeks were people of the concept. They had few laws but they had ideas, and through their ideas and philosophies, they changed their relationships.

The shamans work with perceptual states of consciousness and awareness in order to come to ayni. Let me provide an example to explain how it can work. There is an African tribe where a song is created for each newborn child. The mother sings the song and the entire village learns the song of each child, singing it with love on occasion as the child grows. Later on, if that person comes out of balance and does something that does not serve the village, like stealing or an act of violence, the entire village comes together encircling the culprit and sings their song. The village does this in order to remind them of their true nature and bring them back into balance. Instead of perceiving the person as malevolent and in need of punishment or removal from the village, their perception of both the person and the event allows them to keep order and harmony in the village, in spite of the contrast.

In the Western approach to errant behavior, we say that a bad person has broken the law and lock them up, eradicating them from the village altogether. We perceive them as just plain bad or evil, according to our moral and statutory laws—and this perception maintains the disharmony in our village. Our laws don't deter another from becoming out of balance and acting on it, which is why despite our Western approach, crime is rising and prisons are overflowing. We will discuss this in more detail in the section on Justice.

I mentioned earlier that the main source of all pathologies we face as humans come from this concept called judgment. This notion that we are able to determine what is good and what is bad—not only for ourselves, but also for everyone else—is fundamentally flawed. We have no way of knowing whether an event that is judged as "bad" today, is not part of a bigger picture that unfolds in the future, that can turn out to be "good". And it follows that we cannot know if that "good" event doesn't ultimately lead to the next "bad" thing, and on and on in an exercise of futility. There is a story of a Zen monk in a village where a young man has received a horse for his birthday. One of the villagers says to the monk, "how good, what a fortunate boy," and the monk replies, "maybe, maybe not." Some days later, the young man falls off of the horse and breaks his leg, and the villager says to the monk, "how terrible," and the monk replies "maybe, maybe not." Then a war breaks out and all of the young men of the village are drafted into battle, except the young man because his leg is broken, and the villager says to the monk, "how fortunate for the boy," and the monk replies, "maybe, maybe not."

The real irony is that even our most popular book says, "Judge not," and at the same time our religious, political, and social structure is based on judgments and laws, and our government is mostly run by lawyers and other lawmakers. Along with these laws, we have morals that are also simply judgments based on a majority. We tend to be very moralistic, even though for the most part we are not very moral. It is important to note that morals, like man made laws, are often arbitrary and temporary. For example, less than one hundred years ago it was considered completely moral in the United States to keep women from voting; now it is considered immoral to keep women from voting. Shamans are amoral, meaning that they follow a code of ethics that is in harmony with nature, love, empowerment, and freedom, but they have no need to create morals, law, or judgments over themselves or others.

We are going to delve deeper into this, but first, let me clarify what often comes up when I start talking about this judgment with my fellow humans. There is a difference between discernment and judgment. Discernment is critically important to our "play" here as physically focused discrete pieces of Source. Discernment is what drives our choices, which are in turn what keeps life force

151

flowing through our physical bodies. With discernment, we see someone doing something, or an opportunity just shows up, and we say, "I don't want to do that; they can do it if they want, but I wouldn't want to." On the other hand, with judgment we say, "I don't want to do that, and they shouldn't either, they are bad or wrong for doing that, or that opportunity shouldn't even exist, for it is bad." Do you see the difference? Discernment allows for the wonderful diversity we came here for in the first place, whereas judgment would have everyone be and do exactly like you. You may like a world like that for about three days, but then you would be bored out of your mind.

I know that there are a lot more implications and questions that arise from the proposal of eradicating judgment, and we will address those in detail later. Furthermore, it would go against my whole premise to eradicate anything. Therefore, judgment will still be a part of our diversity. And we can even avoid judging judgment. But, for the improvement of your experiences as well as all of our relationships, choosing not to judge more often, or to put it in the positive—to be more allowing—can be helpful.

In relationships, there are really only two states of being and interacting; namely, love or fear. All other states are subsets of these two. For example, anger, judgment, resentment, grief, greed, violence, and so on are all fear-based; and, appreciation, compassion, joy, allowing, forgiveness, kindness, and so on are all love-based. The interesting thing is that you cannot be in both states at the same time. When the great teachers talk about overcoming or having no fear, they are not talking about the kind of fear that says, "See dinosaur...run!" Instead, they are talking about the kind of fear that keeps us out of the preferred states of love, the kind of fear that we are consciously or unconsciously choosing without any real dinosaurs in sight.

When we are not choosing fear, we are resting in our natural state of love. In other words, consciousness, the One, the Universe, is love. I grew up hearing "God is Love," but now I understand what that means—that the Source of all creation is this stream of pure-positive energy or light that is constant well-being. Thus, the only way to experience anything other than love is by blocking that light or stream of well-being. Moreover, that source of well-being is always available to us for the asking without itself being judging or conditional. Therefore, to the shamans there is no independent source of fear or evil. There is no dark switch on the wall that fills the room with thick black stuff when you turn it on. Instead, there is only the blocking of the Source, or the turning off of the light switch. That is why the shamans say that evil only lives in the hearts and minds of humans.

Evil is just a word or label that is often associated with a persona (since Westerners tend to anthropomorphize everything), which is assigned to represent the state or act of blocking or resisting our Source. This blocking may occur by a conscious or unconscious (Energetic, Mythic, or Psycho-spiritual) choice. The Western myth of a being what we call "the Devil," is just an external personification of that part of ourselves that is blocked from the light; for the unblocked part Westerners have assigned a being they call God. And in their warrior fashion, they've created a battle between the Devil and God that they play out in all aspects of their lives. Of course, each person has the freedom to choose the belief that such independent personas do exist, and the Universe will provide evidence to support his belief. This is why every religion is right. This is also why I would not attempt to change anyone's beliefs if he does not want to change. But when my clients come to me asking to help change what they are experiencing in their reality, then I let them know that they are free to change their beliefs, and I am happy to help, so that their reality follows suit.

I've had many clients that were suffering in their lives because of the very real events and deeply held beliefs around the notions of evil and evildoers. Several clients have experienced satanic ritual abuse as young children, for example. In a culture that has been disempowering for so long, some desperate people have decided that this type of ritual around stealing energy from others with the help of an all-powerful being is the only way to get their power back. And even though others perpetrated these acts on them early in their lives, my clients were finding ways to continue the ritual abuse to themselves into their adulthood, usually self-inflicted but still considered to be from an evil source. Some of the key beliefs associated with this deep wounding are "I am abused and it is my fault," "I am evil," "I am a bad person," "I deserve to be punished," "I am a victim," and "I am powerless." For these people, there was no longer an external evil enemy to do battle with, so the battle continued to rage inside of them until the healing could be conducted on all four levels, and the world could be made safe for them, and they could be made safe for themselves and the world again.

Several of my clients were children of survivors of the Holocaust or had experienced it directly in their past lives. Others that I have worked with, like the Armenians and Native Americans, have seen similar acts of violence and genocide. The deep wounding of these

154

horrific events has come through not only on the ancestral level, but also often as a result of direct trauma from exposure to their family's or friend's psychological issues and internal perpetuation of these events. A few of the core beliefs of these cultures were directly related to my clients' own personal experiences and stories going back thousands of years, and thereby continued to affect my clients in the present. A few of these core beliefs were: "I am persecuted," "I have to fight Evil," and "I am one of God's chosen people." Since the Universe gives us evidence that makes our beliefs right, you can see how difficult and conflicting reality had become for these clients and friends. Regardless of their successes in life, the battle needed to continue, and there needed to be evil enemies to do battle with, and in satisfying their roles as God's chosen, it was entirely their responsibility to fulfill that expectation. A good example of this was a Jewish client of mine, a successful and extremely wealthy businessman, who was being sued by another company under the false claim that he had essentially stolen their idea. That lawsuit set up a battle that would go on for years, and eat away at the peace of mind that he thought his success would have brought to him and his family. So, although perpetrators like Hitler are gone, they continue to be replaced by other "evil" characters. The goal of my Jewish friends and my goal are one and the same – "never again." Let's not have a world where genocide is considered an option, and where we must continually battle those who would prejudge and favor that on either side.

The only difference between the Shamanic approach and the traditional religious or cultural approach is in the method used to achieve the goal. In the Shamanic techniques, we heal ourselves, change the beliefs that no longer serve our goal, and forgive and allow the healing, freedom, and equality of those who would be deemed our "evil enemies." When we put down our weapons that are pointed inward and outward, there is no longer a need for enemies. We must put the cart before the horse so to speak by doing the internal healing work and dreaming the new reality into being instead of reacting to and acting on the currently manifested reality. The new peaceful warrior approach is to find out where the light is blocked within us, and simply turn on the light switch, or remove the block. There is no need to engage in battle. And when there is no need to engage in battle, no enemies manifest.

Now it is true in my experience that there are beings both physical and non-physical that are so blocked, so much in fear, so wounded, so angry, that they are constantly lashing out and acting in ways that some find it easy to call them evil, possessed by the devil, or at least nasty. And the healing process for these beings can be monumental, which makes it even easier for us to be tempted to just throw in the towel and do everything we can just to banish them; but still that is not the ultimate solution. Ultimately, they and the experiences they bring us will just continue to repeat in other ways. Even these beings ultimately need love, healing, and reconnection to Source. In my experience, this is the only real and lasting solution to the problem that so many in the world call evil. Therefore, regardless of how we believe it or describe it, we are essentially all on the same page in terms of wanting less "evil" in the world.

So in terms of our most difficult relationships, since there is no "rule of assertion" in the Universe, the most heinous acts cannot be blamed on someone (or some evil principle) that would be doing them just for fun. Instead, they are always an opportunity to unblock the light or heal and bring back the true nature of the Source, which is love and well-being. It is interesting to note that even within our Western mythologies a more accurate portrayal of God's highest angel "Lucifer," which means *bringer of light*, may be as a representation of the healing process. The Inka have a similar character in their mythology called Huascar, who is dedicated to helping us bring that which is unconscious and is blocking the light, our Source, into consciousness so that it can be healed and no longer blocks the light. Thus, Huascar actually represents a benevolent principle in their mythology – helping to connect us more fully to the Source by showing us where we are blocked and assisting in the purging process.

Huascar, like Lucifer, lives in the underworld, the world of lost parts of our soul, a dark and subconscious world where the fires deep in the Earth serve to burn away impurities. As shamans, we journey to that world to retrieve the lost souls and help them heal more quickly, so that they can be returned and make our clients whole again. In Western culture, we have described this world as Hell, or Purgatory, where we think souls go all at once and only after a person dies. In Tibetan lore, it is referred to as the Bardo plains. We have accepted the fact that it can take a very long time to get out of there, and that there is nothing you can do about it once you are there. But if you work hard enough, and battle long enough, and perform certain acts of repentance, or accept Jesus as your savior while you are still alive, or do whatever your Imam, guru, priest, or Rabbi tell you, then you may not have to go there – and they are made right. It is an interesting spin on the ancient and core Shamanic practices that are more interactive and graceful acts of power to keep your soul parts with you in the light of

Source (Heaven). Again, we all have the freedom to choose, and I support whatever works best for any given person.

Shamans work with clients, and use purging or cleansing elements such as fire and stones, to help get the job done while we are still alive, which is why I think Jesus was a shaman, and why it makes sense that he called himself a son of God. The word, Inka, means child of the Sun (Source of Light), so when you put it all together, the Western stories are not that far off from the older indigenous stories. The biggest difference is that to the shamans, it is still happening today, and to the Church, it happened two thousand years ago. According to the Church, Jesus was the only shaman ever and the Church is the only way to access his healing work now, even though, according to the stories of Jesus, he would reprimand such thought. These notions have taken away our direct relationship with God and nature, disempowering us from our own potential.

Furthermore, we are told that we are not worthy to heal ourselves. I remember every Sunday in church reciting one of the rote prayers that goes, "Lord, I'm not worthy to receive you, but only say the word and I shall be healed." The Church's notion of Hell and its eternal fires and suffering is why we may have such a hard time with that Devil character and associate him with all the "bad" experiences we have on Earth, and think that the only way out is to side with the Church and God in this epic battle. Moreover, if someone is not on the side of your particular Church and God, the only one true and legitimate one, then they must be on the side of the enemy.

As this view of good and evil has been applied to relationships over the last several thousand years, it has been tested repeatedly and proven to fail. The conclusion is that it is an ineffective approach to point our fingers at someone externally, or some aspects of ourselves internally, and say they are "evil", or influenced by the Devil, and therefore need to be punished or eradicated; and furthermore, that we must rely on our religious institutions to do it for us. It seems to be an easy, yet ultimately disempowering way out, and just perpetuates the self-righteousness that leads to more battle and war.

There is an old story of a great master teacher and one of his students. The story goes that the student decided to separate himself from the teacher and become a teacher himself, developing his own faction based on some disagreements about the teachings. In order for the student to feel confident and gain a following, he began to berate his old teacher and grew to even despise him. It came to a point where the student decided he must kill his teacher to achieve dominance and teach his way. Along a remote path, the student ambushed the teacher and ran him through with a sword. In his last dying words to his student, in a gentle and loving way, the teacher told him to go straight ahead and not to return down the path the way he had come, otherwise the people would know that he had killed him. The teacher, knowing that his death was only another transition of life, told the student this because he knew that the people who were not enlightened about death would seek revenge and more bloodshed would be perpetuated. He wanted the student to be the only one that knew so that only one person would suffer from this deed instead of many.

While the Shamanic approach is certainly not easy, as it requires a significant amount of healing work and taking personal responsibility for seeing that this work gets done, the results and evidence of its benefits, in terms of people quickly finding true peace, harmony, and compassion in their relationships, is promising for the world. And it really is only as difficult as we choose to perceive it to be. At some point, we will get used to this seemingly new approach and practices, and they will become natural for us once again.

The Fifth Opportunity – Shadow Work

One of the most powerful, but at the same time peaceful and graceful, Shamanic approaches to dealing with and solving difficult relationship issues is an act of power and love called "shadow work." With shadow work, all relationships, even the ones we have with people we just see on TV or in the news, offer a tremendous opportunity for growth given our largely un-healed state of existence at this time. To the wholly free and powerful, such as Q'ero shamans, the Bodhisattvas, and other truly free and empowered humans, this doesn't really apply all that much. This is because they have already shined a light into all the nooks and crannies of their psyches and their myths, exposing and embracing that which was previously hidden.

Shadow work goes like this: If there is anybody, any situation, or any behavior that really bothers you, pushes your buttons, or makes you angry or envious, it is an exaggeration of a part of you that you do not see, do not want to see, or are battling to eradicate. It is called shadow work because the light of our conscious awareness has not yet shone upon it. In the Western psychological approach, Carl Jung was the first to address the shadow as a part of our psyche that we reject because of fear or ignorance. These shadow situations will often manifest in groups and in multiple different mechanisms and situations. For example, several people in your life might be expressing a lack of support for you, and at the same time, you're having mechanical troubles with your house or car, and/or you might be experiencing a sore back or other injury where your body isn't supporting you either.

By the Rule of Resonance, the Universe (which includes you) has brought into your experience the players and behaviors that you are unconsciously or consciously judging and doing battle with in yourself, because of the tremendous energy broadcast that your inner battle sends out. These people and situations usually come into your experience in an exaggerated way so that you will notice them. There are also two types of shadow, the ones that represent behaviors we abhor and the ones that represent behaviors we adore and may be envious of. So those jerks, morons, criminals, beautiful people, and saints that continue to cross your path and trigger you, are actually the greatest gifts to yourself. This is because the shadow is otherwise the most difficult thing to heal, simply because you usually can't find it on your own, or when you do, the brain talks you out of looking at it and embracing it.

The solution or healing of shadow is very simple, but can be very difficult. To work with shadow, you simply notice when you are bothered or triggered, either with anger or disgust, or with overwhelming admiration or envy. Then when you are over the initial emotional brunt of it, like maybe later that day when you are lying in bed, try to think of a time when you might have exhibited the same behavior or have had the potential to express the behavior even if you stopped yourself. Look for it to be usually in a far less exaggerated way than what you observed. If you can't think of a specific instance, just imagine a situation or set of circumstances when you might be able to express it. For example, if violence bothers you, what would it take for you to act violently—maybe if someone were threatening your loved one? Or for other examples, when would you cheat, or lie, or act harshly toward someone, even in a little way to protect them or teach them? On the other hand, in the case of the envy shadow, when have you acted with unconditional kindness, or said something profound, or showed courage? We could go on and on with examples, but if you look closely enough at your whole life, which is the Shamanic practice called "recapitulation," you will find your own shadow situations, however subtle they may be.

Now here is the biggest trick and paradox of shadow work. Once you have found your shadows, you must consciously and deliberately embrace and love those aspects of you. Often people will feel they have completed their shadow work just by recognizing their shadows, but they haven't taken the next step of actually embracing them, and therefore are still experiencing their effects. It is important to fully acknowledge and love these aspects by recognizing that they will always be a part of you as long as you are in physical human form. You cannot get rid of them regardless of how much battle and discipline you throw at them. Moreover, the very act of trying to get rid of them is causing the vibration/frequency in your energy field that continues to attract the exaggeration in the first place. So the amazingly great thing is that once you embrace those parts of you, the external experiences stop. In other words, no person, event, or behavior will bother you anymore. In fact, either the person playing the role for you will appear to change, or you just won't cross paths with them or that particular behavior anymore. Or, when you are watching them give a speech on TV, you will be neutral or even delighted, knowing that it is for the benefit of many others who are still wrestling with their shadow.

Another point is that people in groups or masses can experience the same shadows in the form of world leaders and public figures. This is what I call collective shadow. Once the critical mass of people in a group embrace that shadow aspect of themselves, then the one playing the role will be replaced. It is the Rule of Resonance acting on a collective scale.

What can make shadow work difficult is the fact that you might not want to look at it or admit it; after all, that is why it is shadow in the first place. Secondly, we are afraid that if we embrace it, somehow we are condoning it, and it will take over and we will become some kind of monster. But this simply is not true. The paradox is that even as we embrace the shadows, we will always exhibit our dominant true nature, which is harmony, allowing, and light.

I like to use the example of going into the cookie store, where we do really well with choosing what we want and allowing the rest. I'll go in and the person behind the counter asks what I would like. I look through the selection of cookies and I really don't like the peanut butter ones, cannot even stand the smell of them. Now what I tell the person is that I'll have the chocolate chip with nuts. What I don't do is point at the peanut butter ones and say, "Oh my God, I don't want those, you have to get rid of those before they take over," and then gather friends with picket signs, and organize groups across the country to march in front of every cookie store in the hopes of someday eradicating those horrible peanut butter cookies. No, I embrace the fact that in this diverse world, there is room for all kinds of cookies and I just have to choose the ones I like and allow or embrace the ones that others like. The paradox is that the more you focus your attention in battle against something you don't like, the bigger it gets in your experience. This is true for all external battles, like the war against poverty, the war against terrorism, the war against drugs, the war against dictators, the war against war... and the only reason there are these external battles that never end is because of our internal battles. This is where embracing the shadow and putting down your weapons is so effective and necessary for complete healing to occur on a personal and global scale.

Let me finish this piece on shadow work with a personal example. For several years, I was practicing the yogic traditions that are designed to lead us to enlightenment. It was a much-disciplined practice with hours of study, meditation, contemplation, vegetarian diet, specific exercises, and celibacy. These are the practices of what is sometimes referred to as the Sanyasin, renunciant, or monk. The idea is that you completely transcend the ego, body urges, and negative emotions, and attain a state of awareness of the One, and unconditional love for all. You can see that, deliberately or not, it sets up internal battles with many of the natural characteristics of being human, like fear, anger, sensuality, and so on. Well, after a few years, I felt that I had actually won the battles, I was able to get through my difficult work-day with great equanimity, actually feeling unconditional love for most of those around me, and even the ones that cut me off in traffic. I had no sex drive, no ambition for wealth and recognition, and I felt fearless. I was in bliss most of the time, completely oblivious

of the natural tendencies that I had "transcended" and the battles
smoldering deep in my subconscious. I really felt like a saint,
and my presence around most others had a noticeably calming
effect, the love was contagious. I could have donned a robe and
moved to a cave or ashram; in fact, I actually began to ask
myself the question as to whether I should go ahead and do that,
because there wasn't much use in hanging around the world where
I wasn't really participating. The other option was of course to just
go ahead and leave my body. The answer I came up with for
myself, since I was only about 26 years old at the time, was to just
stick around, participate in the world again in somewhat "normal
fashion," and then do the same thing when I'm about 87 and check
out at 90, since I knew it could be done.

In the meantime, I was really into this new found sainthood and I
began to have some people, which were primarily my bosses at
work, exhibit behavior towards me that could best be described as
abusive. To me they seemed mean, harsh, overly critical,
unreasonable, gruff, and even violent at times. Each of three
bosses, as I tried to escape them, became increasingly
greater exaggerations of abusiveness, in my experience anyway.
By the third, I was getting very desperate and confused. I would
try to get consensus from others that worked for him, but they
would just say things like "What do you mean, he's nice, he's cool,
etc." I tried to love him unconditionally anyway, and be soft-
spoken, kind, and cooperative, none of which helped change him
(as if I could). Finally, I learned about shadow work from a set of
tapes that my great friend and benefactor, Dean, gave me from the
book "Dark Side of the Light Chasers" by Debbie Ford.

So one night, I lay in bed, trying really hard to remember the times I acted a little harsh or abusive like my boss; well, sad to say at the time (but with a hearty laugh now), it wasn't that hard to find. And when I realized that part of me had always been there and continued to be even through "sainthood," or "Siddhahood," I just accepted that I can be like that sometimes and it is okay, and in fact it may even serve at times; and, I love myself and forgive myself anyway. This is all I had to do, it took about 15 minutes, and it was done. Roughly two weeks after that night, my boss left to another job and I got a new boss who was the sweetest, most supportive, and generous guy I had ever worked with. And since that time, nine years ago as of this writing, I have not had the experience of running into or being triggered by an abusive person.

And here is the real kicker, if I wasn't absolutely convinced of the power of this work already: One year after the old boss had left I ran into him at a party, fully expecting the same confrontational experience, and instead he smiled, gave me a big hug, and asked how I was doing with great warmth and sincerity. He was friendly and cool, like everyone was saying in the first place. It was unbelievable, or as my first real healer, Sridhar, would say, "believable!" I've since seen it work over and over, both with clients and in my personal experience.

One way to remember to do the shadow work is to think that when you are pointing your finger at someone else, there are three fingers pointing back at you. However, the real key here is that it is not about judging or blaming yourself for the shadow, it is about forgiving, accepting, allowing, embracing, and even loving that little piece of you. It will never take over; in fact, it will even diminish in your behavior. Remember, what you resist persists, what you push against gets bigger, and what you embrace disappears.

Marriage or Life Partnering, Family and Friends

Let's jump right into the big relationships of marriage and family, or partnering if you prefer. Marriage, by definition, is a legal contract that varies greatly across cultures. Which I mention as it ties into our myth as people of the precept. Other types of family and friendship relationships differ from marriage mainly in the fact that they are not contractually bound and therefore make it easier to be unconditional and allowing; but all of these types of relationships have blurred boundaries, and so many of the issues and opportunities overlap. Mutual partnerships, such as marriage, family, and friends, offer the greatest opportunity to work with the five reasons for relationships. This is mainly because you're making a commitment, whether contractually or not, to work things through for the sake of long-term security and certainty, and not just to keep running away from the healing opportunities at hand. Another way to look at it is Joseph Campbell's quote, "if you don't learn it, you marry it," and, even if you're on partner number three, or career number three, you are still married to the "it."

So first, to create some contrast, let's look at how the traditional Western idea of marriage has fared. So far, the divorce rate is about fifty percent, not counting divorce by death (deliberate or not). And how many of the other fifty percent would get divorced if they could—if they didn't have some secondary benefit or threat (such as money, kids, fear of being alone or what others might say, or self-punishment) keeping them in the marriage? Moreover, there are many couples that are still together but not really fulfilling the contract because they are using forms of escape like workaholism. I don't know what the percentage of actual working marriages turns out to be, but it's not looking like a successful institution from the strictly traditional view and practice. There seems to be room for new approaches and/or a greater acceptance of alternative approaches that are working.

Then there is the whole concept of raising children in a stable environment with a mommy and daddy, which perpetuates the myth that we have to get married to have or raise children, or visa versa. How many married couples actually have the wisdom and training necessary to serve as examples, teachers, and healers for these souls they have chosen to take care of? So often, children are used to fill a hole that needed to be healed properly, such as self-esteem issues, lack of support and nurturing, an excuse to fit in to society or have power, or to add to a partnership that is dysfunctional to begin with. We could go on and on with what works and what doesn't, and there are many books on the subject, but for our purpose of making the contrast conscious in order to create a new vision, this is enough. Po Bronson, in his best-selling book, "Why Do I Love These People?" cites statistics that show that the current, somewhat dismal, situation in marriage and families is not just a modern phenomenon, but dates back hundreds of years. In fact, believe it or not, it is better now than it ever was!

I have noticed time and time again when working with couples and individuals on relationship issues that there are two fundamental types of relationships that belong in two distinct categories: business on the one hand and friends and family on the other. Problems seem to arise from the blurring of the boundaries of these types of relationships. This is mainly due to the fact that we engage in business for most of our waking hours and have difficultly switching that off for the rest of our waking hours.

Business relationships are what I call transactional relationships. This means that we relate to each other in terms of a balance sheet and fair market values. For example, if I give you a service or product for a certain amount of time or quantity, then you give me something of equal value in return so that our balance sheet remains even. Everything we do in the business world involves financial statements, balance sheets, liabilities versus assets and return on investment. If we allow this business type transactional relationship to spill over to the realm of family and friends, then in addition to money and services, we are now measuring and attempting to balance our energy, love or appreciation, and emotions.

For example, one working husband was coming to the breaking point with his stay at home wife and their two young children. The fundamental problem from the husband's point of view was that his wife was spending more money than she was making up for—a purely transactional viewpoint. His wife was on the liability side of the balance sheet instead of the asset. Of course, this tension was causing a rift that spilled over into the emotional and physical aspects of the relationship, creating even more liability or deficit. So in the husband's business oriented mind, he was thinking of divorcing her in the way that he would think of having a lay-off or divesting of a draining part of the business. The only alternative in his mind would be for his wife to make more money or be less emotionally or Energetically draining, to balance out the transaction of their marriage.

Let's contrast this example with a loving relationship that is more ideally suited for friends and family. In this relationship, the commodities are unconditional support, sharing, joy, laughter, and physical and emotional pleasure, and there is no way to quantify those and put them in a balance sheet. You engage in this kind of relationship just for the fun of it, not to win, lose, or break-even. You do it because the alternative is to be completely alone in the world, devoid of any relationships. Interestingly, but of course not surprisingly, the husband in my example didn't view his dog in terms of a transactional relationship because in general we don't deal with dogs in business as we do with other human beings. So it is easier to keep the two types separate in this case.

As the gap between the transactional and loving relationship narrows, the joys of unconditional giving and receiving, joy, laughter, and pleasure get replaced by the sadness, pain, doubt, fear, and despair that can come with a dysfunctional business. The ideal is to be able to leave the transactional relationship in the office and switch to the loving relationship model with our friends and family, and if anything, let that model spill over more into our business oriented world. Being less influenced by the pressures and expectations around us helps; and we have already discussed how Shamanic processes accomplish this.

Concerning close friends and family, there is always the opportunity for drama, and it is not always pleasing. The way we've been taught—our normal reaction—is to blame and judge, either them or ourselves. We tend to get caught up in these cycles of drama and the resulting battles. We think that we will be happy if only the other just stops doing what they are doing or goes away.

Or we believe that by exerting our influence or asserting ourselves physically, we can somehow force the situation to be favorable for us. This is particularly evident in the way many parents attempt to interfere with the Rule of Resonance by giving a child something they are screaming for, or holding back something the child had naturally manifested, for the convenience of the parent. In fact, the way our parents have been raising us traditionally for generations is one of the primary reasons that we have unlearned these basic rules of the Universe.

What happens is that from the start of our lives, we associate our behavior with the pleasure or displeasure of those around us, primarily our parents. So we develop the belief that we are responsible for the experiences of others. We learn that we are responsible for their happiness through our actions; and there couldn't be anything farther from how the Universe actually works. Now, since it is our nature to want to please others, we place on ourselves the burden of jumping through as many hoops as we can to keep everyone around us happy. And since this is impossible, and since we cannot and do not create in another's experience, we begin to see ourselves as failures, or fundamentally flawed, or at worst evil, and grow more and more bitter, resentful, and distrustful of the world. There are many solutions however, and many examples of successful family and friend relationships that we can appreciate.

Vision for Marriage, Life Partnerships, Family, and Friends
My vision is that we get on the path of our own personal healing early on in life so that by the time we are capable of, and have the urge to choose a partner or mate, we do it more from the place of power and freedom. Our compatibility comes from our self-

171

awareness/self-honesty, playfulness, and from the basis of the four core opportunities (and hopefully not so much of the fifth opportunity or shadow work). We understand that it is our choice and responsibility alone to be happy or not. And if we end up choosing a partner and it turns out mostly to be an opportunity for further healing, ala Joseph Campbell, we then have the freedom, support, and understanding to end or shift the partnership gracefully once the healing is accomplished.

We understand that all of those that have come into our experience, and us into theirs, are a result of the Rule of Resonance, whether pleasing or painful. Moreover, we see these relationships as an opportunity to enjoy the drama, whether pleasing or painful, and become the witness when necessary so that we can remain mostly light and playful. We also recognize that many of these relationships have been in place through lifetimes and in between lifetimes, and that the situations may not be entirely understandable or resolved from only the Psycho-spiritual or physical layers; but that these relationships may need to be healed on the Energetic and Mythic levels as well through Shamanism and ceremony.

Notes on Your Vision for Marriage, Life Partnerships, Family, and Friends:

We allow for the possibility and support of marriages and partnerships to take on unlimited diverse forms and duration while always remembering and maintaining the core reasons for our interactions and relationships, rather than just attempting to preserve them. So for example, instead of relationship for the sake of the survival of the relationship, it's relationship for the experience of unconditional love and ecstatic union (sex). If children become a part of our life deliberately and we have done much of our healing work, then we continue to raise them based mostly on example, and in harmony with our core desires. If it wasn't from our clarity, we don't know enough to be reasonable examples or learn quickly from their wisdom, or we end up compromising our true desires and true needs, then we consider allowing others to raise them who do have the desire and wisdom to be fully engaged in that process.

In some of the least-Western-influenced indigenous cultures, the young and fertile men and women mate to give birth (usually in their mid-teens); and then the grandmothers and grandfathers (usually early to mid 30's on up) of the village are the ones who raise and educate the children. This keeps the functionality of the relationships and village in good balance and sustainable. Of course, in most Western cultures, this situation would look quite different as the family and village dynamics have changed substantially over the last several hundred years. Thus, we would probably need to start a whole new cycle of education, healing, trust, and valuing of children and their teachers and caretakers – the elders.

Parent/Child Relationships

The parent/child relationship is unique and dynamic over the course of a lifetime. For the first stages of life, the parent has the responsibility for feeding, nurturing, and assuring the safety of the child as she begins to get reacquainted with the physical world. On at least a subconscious level, even before a baby is born, the soul in the fetus's body is taking in the core Energetic influences of the parents as well as some of their Mythic, Psycho-spiritual, and physical influences. As a baby and toddler, these external influences become increasingly multi-layered (i.e. Energetic, Mythic, Psycho-spiritual, and physical) and expand beyond just the parents. To the infant, the whole world is an extension of her body. As the child grows into puberty, the influences come increasingly from outside the family, and the child develops his/her independence in every respect. As the stage of puberty passes, the natural impulse is to become completely independent of the parent/child relationship.

Most indigenous cultures have very clear Energetic and Mythic rituals for making an elegant and complete transition between stages. In this case, it is the rite of passage that frees the parents from their responsibilities and clearly assigns the Earth and Sun as the child's true and only mother and father. A new way of being in the world, and relating to each other begins for this new adult and her parents. The parents are completely off the hook, and the parent/child relationship becomes a friendship. Today we have religious rites (that have been repeated for thousands of years), but our modern lives have not allowed us to fully engage and understand the meaning of them in the original context. For example, Confirmation and Bar Mitzvah ceremonies are now mostly seen as excuses to receive gifts and demand even more from our parents, as opposed to being a Mythic journey from dependence to responsibility that has a very real and practical application that requires specific Energetic work. Without these religious rites, our rites of passage become our first bra, or the first time we get to drive the car, or our first beer. To regain these meaningful rites of passage, we need to do more than understand the old Mythic ceremonies—we must create new ones with what we have available to us here and now.

Another good example of the loss of the meaning of Mythic ceremonies is related to the dying process, which is often a big part of the parent/child relationship (as well as many other relationships). In the Catholic tradition, the priest says a prayer, bestows a blessing, and then makes the sign of the cross over the forehead and the heart (only two of the chakras). For the most part, we have forgotten the real reasons for these steps—steps that are just a watered down version of the original Shamanic techniques and wisdom that has formed the basis for all religions. The Shamanic version of this death rite involves the processes of recapitulation and life review, which allow us both to forgive those we have blamed for wronging us and to forgive ourselves for those times that we blamed ourselves for wronging others. We then take the time to say, "I love you" to our loved ones, because it is very difficult to do so from the non-physical realms. This rite is not just a memorized prayer, but instead, an active and participatory process that also involves removing and cleansing the Energetic threads related to those engagements. Then, when the dying person takes his or her last breath, the shaman disengages the luminous energy body from all of the chakras with counterclockwise motions in a great spiral ending at the seventh, crown, chakra so that the soul passes from there into the eighth chakra and on to the light of the spirit world. Not until the soul has completely left the body, does the shaman make the sign of the cross over all of the chakras, so that the soul does not try to return and attach itself to the decaying body. By contrast, in some cases, the Catholic priest may be sealing the soul in the body by prematurely crossing the chakras, thereby contributing to the phenomenon of haunted cemeteries where the departed and confused souls are still attached to their decaying bodies. Fortunately, like birth, most deaths go just fine since we naturally know how to die. It is just for the one in ten that has trouble with these processes that it is nice to have someone around who knows what she is doing and can assist, like the OB/GYN doctor at the time of birth, and the shaman at the time of death.

These are the Mythic death rites, which are really the life rites, because we don't want to die with unfinished business that may become the death that stalks us and claims us unconsciously time and time again, lifetime after lifetime. By doing these rites, our souls become unfettered, and can be claimed fully by life. It is the completely unfettered soul that has the opportunity to become what the Buddhists call a Bodhisattva, which is someone who comes into the physical world completely conscious of who they are, their luminous nature, and why they came, and is available to help others who are asking to achieve the same.

Vision for the Parent/Child Relationship
My vision for the parent/child relationship is that prospective parents have been educated and healed to the extent that they have a clear understanding of who they are, how and why souls desire to come into physical bodies, and why they are choosing to become a

parent. In this vision, the parents also elicit the help of wise people in their community in the care and education of their children. The parents understand and honor the unique desires and gifts of the soul that has come forth and do everything possible to nurture and support the child's unique path. The parents understand and practice teaching by example—and recognize that there may be much that the child can teach them, that this child may even be more evolved than them, and therefore ready to bring whole new perspectives, technologies, approaches, and beliefs to the world.

The parents offer many choices and allow the child to choose freely, giving unconditional love and support; and this includes allowing choices to work on the Energetic healing of imprints in the child's soul that might have been brought forward into this life, since Shamanic healing can take place at any age. The parents recognize and work with all layers of existence from the beginning of the pregnancy until the child is released at adulthood. This means that the parents provide not only a nurturing and safe physical environment, but also understand the influence of energies, emotions, thoughts, and myth on the child, and engage the Mythic layer with ceremonies and rites of passage for both themselves and the children.

The parents have a clear understanding of the Rules of Resonance and Receptivity and allow the child to learn these freely, even through trial and error if necessary. The parents have a clear understanding that the children of today are the future parents, and that the parents of today are the future children, and so on in an eternal cycle that knows no death; so that what we do for the children, we eventually reap the benefits from as well. The parents know that children respond the way the Universe responds, because they just came from the Universe; and therefore the parents know how to communicate effectively, in a positive and inclusive way filled with openness, clarity, nurturing, support, forgiveness, allowing, with gentle guidance mostly through example. The parents help the child to understand that the child's nature is good, and that the child is not responsible for the happiness of those around her. We will address more on the raising of our children in the section on Education.

Notes on Your Vision for the Parent/Child Relationship:

Work, Community, National, and Global Relationships

Like marriages, relationships on the larger scales of work, community, national, and global situations are often governed by legal contracts or treaties. And anytime you take beings that have come forth on the basis of freedom, for the purpose of joy and the resulting growth and expansion, and force them into a limited and rigid long-term set of rules, you foster the potential for resentment and rebellion, battles and betrayals, collective psychoses, and Energetic and Mythic wounds.

Shamans are often called upon to help an entire business, village, or country. There are visionaries working on the healing of the relationships of the entire planet, if not even broader reaches. If we apply the five principles of relationships to these broader scales, it is easy to see that, to the extent that we fail on the individual level, we suffer the same repercussions in all of our collective larger-scale endeavors. At work for example, there is often more competition (fear-based), than cooperation (love-based). In our communities, we have judgment or prejudice about the people that we do not know. It is as if we believe they are somehow much different from us, and the Universe makes us right so that our experiences continue to build on our fears of the "unknown." The prejudged often then also turn on themselves and each other until all hope is lost. Or they find hope in desperate clinging to traditions, habits, and external stimulus. This clinging can become a form of suicide if the fear of death becomes less powerful than the fear of judgment and rejection from the community. We often create greater and greater fears to overcome even the fear of death or rejection, in the hopes that the fears force us to work together and help each other; this is often the direction taken with the help of organized religion.

There are huge differences between allowing versus tolerating, and between helping from a place of true nature versus a place of obligation or fear. Tolerating means to have the judgment and the disgust inside, but just hide it. Allowing means seeing equal value in what another has chosen; and therefore, their choice doesn't bother you at all. Allowing gives us the opportunity to help one another from a place of compassion, joy, and non-attachment rather than from a place of fear that we will be punished if we don't help - despite our disgust. And what do we do with those "criminals, misfits, and evil-doers" that we don't know how to help? Reacting from a place of fear, we would just kill them or put them away where we don't have to know that they exist, as we do now. How long can we do this before there is no more available land or money to build and maintain prisons?

Communities become nations, where the victim/perpetrator/rescuer dynamic manifests as genocide, mass-poverty, repression, and war. Freedom fighters are called terrorists and insurgents depending upon whom you're talking to; and, terrorism is called war depending on the size of the budget. War, repression, mass-poverty and genocide come about because people think they know what is better for somebody else and use whatever means to try to prove it, usually justified by the God that is on their side, and wholly driven by the fear that if they tolerate another culture, it will take over.

We all want people to treat others with love, respect, nurturing, fairness, support, and allowing. However, we cannot solve the problem by being the problem, even if we think we are on the righteous side of it. A good example is the notion that the Western way of life is superior to all other ways, now and throughout history. We claim to enjoy the highest quality of life, measured mostly by material possessions, levels of consumption, variety of choices, and longevity, which are quantitative, not qualitative, measures. Nevertheless, there is mounting evidence that our way of life is not sustainable and could come to a crashing halt in the near future. And are we truly happier, more fulfilled, healthier (mentally and physically), and freer than "non-Westerners"? I'll offer this one statistic for thought: the Shuar people living deep in the Amazon Jungle spend 4 hours a day "working" in order to have all that they need and desire to live a full life, including food, shelter, child-rearing, medicine, arts & crafts, song and dance. The remaining 20 hours are free for play and sleep. Contrast that to the average American who has to work 8 –16 hours a day mostly just to survive, and if fortunate, to be able to save enough money to do what the Shuar do, and call it "retirement." Moreover, the Shuar people have been living this way for thousands of years and can continue to live this way indefinitely.

Here is one last note on war. Righteousness (religious or political), victim consciousness, scarcity, and fear permeate both our past and ongoing mythology and have had groups and nations killing each other for thousands of years. And no matter how hard we try—no matter how many battles, how many wars—whatever we are trying to get rid of remains, and often gets bigger. We simply can't build enough prisons or dig enough graves. It doesn't matter if it's a war against poverty, a war against cancer, a war on drugs, a war on terrorism, a war against rogue nations, a war on crime, a war against violence, a war against war, it just hasn't worked. There will always appear to be another battle that is necessary to fight. How many more thousands of years of the warrior approach would it take to figure that out, unless we choose to drop it today?

Vision for Work, Community, National, and Global Relationships

My vision for larger scale relationships is that the healing we achieve as individuals, finds its way into these relationships, such that we understand that allowing, cooperating, leading by example, and being open to the possibility that there may be wisdom and value in all approaches, is the most efficient and effective way to thrive as a species. In this vision, we remember that our organizations are created to serve the people, and that change is okay in order to serve better; and that service is based on sustainable quality of life for all those who would choose it. We understand that innovation can come from cooperation and sharing equally, if not more so, than from competition. We recognize the value of and honor diversity, and encourage and even celebrate it on all levels.

Notes on Your Vision for Work, Community, National, and Global Relationships:

Chapter 7
Education

The majority of our modern education systems and institutions are designed to give us only the basic understanding, information, and techniques to function in a factory-based industrialized society. There is little emphasis on the knowledge and techniques required to thrive and to find our greatest joy in life, let alone to encourage the likes of a Da Vinci, Newton, Einstein, Keller, or Jane Addamsto dream and to create an even better life. Modern institutions have lost sight of the natural and joyous aspects of learning, and seem to have forgotten that we learn best when we are studying that which brings us the greatest joy and passion. Most students in traditional Western educational institutions are forced or coerced into learning and achieving that which external factors deem to be the most important or most fulfilling line of work. The student is left to struggle, not only with trying to learn enough information to fulfill somebody else's choice for their career, but also in determining what they may truly want to do in life. If the student is not impassioned or motivated by joy, then that struggle often creates a vicious cycle of trying to make enough money to buy things to make up for the lost joy. And this all assumes that the student is actually willing to stay in school and graduate in the first place. At the time of writing this book, statistics show that one in four students is dropping out of high school in the United States, amounting to seven thousand dropouts per day. Moreover, a large number of these students who have dropped out are not becoming productive and healthy members of society; instead, they are ending up with serious drug problems and in prisons.

My own story is an example of someone who stayed with the system, although I was disenchanted with the way the system operated both as a student and later as a teacher. My initial goal of learning (once I was old enough to be conscious of it) was simply to get the highest scores and achievements, as anything less would be a failure to my parents, the institution, and society. Then, as I attended college, my goal became to obtain the degree I needed in order to have a secure job doing something that I was good enough at, in which capacity I would hopefully make enough money so that someday I could do what I really wanted to do. Does this sound familiar to you? The problem was that I was so unmotivated and overworked in my job that I squandered or gambled the money on "investments," desperately trying to find relief from my situation as quickly as possible.

I was heavily influenced by the values of the times in which I was growing up. It was during the Space race, so I was drawn towards being an astronaut. This career seemed exciting enough to me at a young age to motivate me towards pursuing a technical field of study. The closest thing that college could offer to me to achieve this goal was Electrical Engineering, or at least that was the safest choice that a NASA engineer had recommended to me at the time. The problem was that the Electrical Engineering curriculum had nothing to do with Space, and so I quickly lost interest in my studies; and, as I grew older, I lost the initial passion around traveling into Space. At least I had a degree that would help me get a job and make good money. Somehow, most likely based on old family myths, I was convinced that work was not meant to be enjoyed anyway.

I could have made so many other choices that I wasn't fully aware of at the time, if I had been encouraged to really look at what I enjoyed doing. The clues were there all along, even going all the way back to primary school, where I loved drawing and social interaction, and through high school where my passion was health and human potential. Had I known that learning and work were supposed to be fun, and that I could even make money having fun, I might have enjoyed a more fulfilling, healthy, productive, and most likely far more abundant twelve years of my young adult life. Nonetheless, I am appreciative of all that I did learn, and how it continues to benefit me even in my Shamanic work.

It is important to acknowledge that the current educational system has produced many very joyful and fulfilling opportunities for people around the world, and there is tremendous value in teaching the basics. Likewise, the University systems do offer the opportunity for passionate and motivated students to expand their knowledge, and not just gather information. However, the process is so often wrought with bureaucratic, political, and financial obstacles that it frequently fosters more warrior-like cutthroat competition and conformity than true innovation and advancement for all of humanity.

Vision for Education
There are primary education systems like the Sudbury Valley School founded in Massachusetts, the Waldorf schools, several evolutions similar to Waldorf, and home schooling programs that are proving to be good models for the new paradigm in education. They tend to honor each individual student's desires and gifts, while also teaching the necessary basics. And in the case of Waldorf, created by Austrian clairvoyant, philosopher, architect,

and inventor Rudolph Steiner, the curriculum is designed to work in harmony with our natural developmental phases, on the Energetic and Mythic, as well as the Psycho-spiritual levels.

My ideal vision for education is to create the resources, whether centralized into a larger institution, or de-centralized into neighborhoods, that allow for enough individual attention and program flexibility to encourage students to learn at their own natural pace and direction, while placing emphasis on having fun and following and expressing their inherent passions. For example, if a child is not having fun with a particular exercise or subject, observe and explore with her to find what she does enjoy doing, and then help her to build on that. Then further support her interests by teaching the basics that will give her the tools to continue to progress towards this joyful work.

This vision for education is kind of a vocational school focus from the very beginning. Education, of course, starts at home with learning the basic rules of the Universe, and encourages exploration and development of our natural desires. In most indigenous cultures, the children have already been trained in, and are doing the work that they enjoy most, before they reach their teens - sometimes as early as five years of age. Some would argue that by starting to work so early in life, the children would not be allowed to be children, but instead that they would be forced to grow up too fast and not be allowed to have fun. But this argument is built on the dysfunctional system that dominates our society, which is that work is not fun. If the child has been educated and is working at something she enjoys, then she never has to grow up and become a miserable adult. Some would argue that a child so young doesn't know what her passion is. I find this similar to the argument that baby boys don't feel the pain of circumcision. Instead, as adults we have not been taught how to honor and encourage a child's passion and feelings. If you offer options to children of any age, and take time to observe their responses and initiatives carefully, you will see that they will make their preferences known, and that they will respond with increasing passion to nurturing encouragement.

The following is the description from the Sudbury Valley School website:

> At Sudbury Valley School, students from preschool through high school age explore the world freely, at their own pace and in their own unique ways. They learn to think for themselves, and learn to use Information Age tools to unearth the knowledge they need from multiple sources. They develop the ability to make clear logical arguments, and deal with complex ethical issues. Through self-initiated activities, they pick up the basics; as they direct their lives, they take responsibility for outcomes, set priorities, allocate resources, and work with others in a vibrant community.

> Trust and respect are the keys to the school's success. Students enjoy total intellectual freedom, and unfettered interaction with other students and adults. Through being responsible for themselves and for the school's operation, they gain the internal resources needed to lead effective lives.

Notes on Your Vision for Education:

Chapter 8
Spirituality and Materialism (or Religion and Science)

I have already covered much ground on this subject, because it has a major influence on our worldview. The conflicts most people have between spirituality and materialism are a result of the notion that the two are separate and irreconcilable. The Shamanic culture recognizes that there really is no separation of spirit and matter, and that even science and religion can share common ground. The battles between science and religion, and those within the sciences and religions are unnecessary under the renewed Shamanic paradigm that I am presenting in this book. Clearly, the most violent of battles across history and to the present day can be traced to the notions fostered by fear-based and righteous factions of religion and science. These systems believe that Creation is finite and closed and that there is only one version of right and wrong and good and evil; and, depending on which side you happen to be on at any given moment, you must be the victim, the perpetrator, or the rescuer.

With many thousands of years of history and hindsight available to an increasingly conscious humanity, it is becoming more and more difficult to ignore the evidence that our age-old worldview, myths, and philosophical approaches have not made things better for us. An entirely new paradigm of ideas and approaches is necessary to make real and lasting changes to our quality of life. I have a number of acquaintances, friends, and clients that have and are holding significant positions in several of the major religious institutions. Each one of them has expressed the need for reform. Likewise, many people working in the sciences are recognizing that something is missing, and that they are searching for it. People on both sides are looking down the chasm of the separation, and few are starting to build bridges, even if not building a bridge threatens the integrity and "safety" of their age-old institutions. Building a bridge is difficult because of our limited view of the existence of only two layers to our being; namely, the Literal and the Psycho-spiritual. Therefore, when you talk about major reforms only from those two levels, crossing the chasm looks more like igniting a revolution; and, most revolutions have not been graceful.

The shaman's approach to bringing religion and science to a place where they both serve humanity together, instead of separating humanity, would be to start at the Energetic and Mythic layers. Many wounds need to be healed, myths rewritten, and fears abated before a more graceful reformation is possible. The irony is that science can be used to support religion, and religion can be used to further science if the two are not seen as enemies. Religion needs to interpret its myths and stories in a way that science can accept; and science needs to be broadened to allow for the possibility that the unseen world is real, and has real impact on the seen world. The paramount principle of religion, namely faith, is maintained under this vision. Faith is equivalent then to a scientific hypothesis. For example, the ultimate statement of faith - ask and it is given - can be tested with the scientific method, and proven. Then faith maintains its relevance in the notion that whatever experience is being asked for will be given in some form or another; and that particular form may remain a mystery until it manifests.

In terms of belief, the importance of a diversity of viewpoints and impassioned believers remains in tact. I would encourage people to believe strongly, and not be easily shaken from their beliefs. But at the same time, no matter how strong your belief is and how much evidence you have to support it, I think it is important to allow others to maintain their own beliefs no matter how much it seems not to serve them. In other words, the paradigm of preaching, soul saving, and religious missions or conquests may not ultimately serve to improve the quality of life on the planet. Moreover, due to the simple fact that diversity and judgment will always exist, people are unlikely to ever agree on one set of beliefs that can be applied to everyone. Any notion that yours is the best belief, simply leads to the kind of "holier than thou" righteousness that begets battles and fear. Even where it seems obvious to you that somebody would benefit greatly by receiving your knowledge and changing their beliefs, unless they are asking for your help it is unlikely that they will receive it as intended. This level of discernment and nonattachment is one of the most valuable aspects of the shaman's training. I remind myself, and others who are prone to the caretaker's archetype, by saying that people cannot hear the answer to the question that they have not asked.

In order to take the fears out of religion and science, all of the available information and knowledge needs to be made accessible to everyone, so that an accurate and sensible understanding can be achieved. More accurate translations and full disclosure of all available scriptures, would allow people to make empowered decisions about the particular religious practices that they resonate with most, and that would serve them best. And this holds true not only for the older religions but also for newer forms of spirituality and science. Truthfully, and to keep this discussion in proper perspective, even the oldest religions started as small cults, that over time grew in popularity and power, while competing cults were destroyed or simply dissolved. Likewise, a small cult today could become one of the world's great religions a thousand years from now.

In my search for and study of the greatest wisdom teachings and explanations of the Universe from around the world, I have found that a universally core principle runs through them all. This core principle is that it is of primary importance to put aside man's agenda-based, fear-based, or overly righteous interpretations of the wisdom teachings in order to live a joyful life. I discovered that the most ancient Shamanic oral traditions seem to get this universal information and knowledge across in the most straightforward and easily understandable manner. After the recent period of many thousands of years, during which the only way that people could remember and practice the core principles of life seemed to be through complex and obscure stories, the universal wisdom seems to be coming through once again in a direct and clear manner through the likes of the teachings of Abraham-Hicks and other modern-day teachers.

There has also been evidence of constant borrowing and paraphrasing of the old stories, which has muddied the teachings of many modern religions. For example, there are ancient pre-Judeo-Christian-Muslim stories of virgin births, angelic and immortal beings, and sacrificial sons. In addition, Greek mythology tells the story of Persephone being visited by Zeus in serpent form to beget the savior Dionysus. Other stories of the sacrificial son and savior come from Egypt's Osiris, Phyrgian's Attis, India's Vishnu, Persia's Mithra, and Greece's Heracles to name a few.

As evidenced by these ancient stories, the major religious institutions as well as the many sects and cults do not have a monopoly on mythmaking or connection to Source. And since these institutions have been created by, and expanded upon by the mind of man, there is obviously room for mistakes. For example, one approach to interpreting the Ten Commandments is as remindful promises rather than instructions. Our current interpretation makes it sound like there is a wrathful and judging God that is keeping score, and will make sure that you suffer for disobeying his commandments. An alternative translation offers simply a wisdom teaching based on experience that says that if you act in a certain way, it will likely bring you the joy that you wish to experience. For example, "Thou shall not kill" becomes "If you allow life, you will find joy (or Heaven on earth)," or even "If you live in joy, you're not likely to kill." Various Buddhist, Hindu, and Muslim traditions, as well, contain their own versions of commandments, judgment, and wrath along with their hierarchical structures.

Let me interject here that I know that some may be offended by how I refer to the Bible and to our Western myths; but I want to make it clear that I recognize and honor all of the wonderful and beautiful teachings in the Bible, and all other Holy Scriptures. I just want to create contrast and awareness so that what has been mostly unconscious can become conscious, which is really the first step in the healing process. Personally, I am a long-time student of the Holy Scriptures, and have always tried to study the original versions (i.e. pre-King James version including the Gnostic Gospels and Dead Sea Scrolls), as well as various translations of these versions in order to get the broadest

SPIRITUALITY AND MATERIALISM

and clearest perspective. I have found that by taking the time to study in this way, there is actually very little, if any, conflict amongst the majority of the religious teachings, or between those teachings and the teachings of my Shamanic training. It also helps to know that the teachings aren't finished; that there are Holy Scriptures and words of God being written and spoken every day through direct connection to that Source. We may find that one thousand years from now, there is a new all time bestseller.

For Christians, Jesus is a living flesh and blood representation of the word of God, as well as their only way into Heaven through their belief *in* him. I have read some translations of the original Aramaic words allegedly spoken by Jesus, which radically change his message. For example, there is an enormous difference if Jesus said, "Believe *in* me, and you shall never die," versus, "Believe me, and you shall never die." The first translation indicates that a simple belief in Jesus as your savior is all you need to enjoy Heaven on Earth, while the second translation indicates that if you use his teachings and follow his example, you will enjoy Heaven on Earth. The first translation seems to require a membership in a cult or religion, while the second maintains your freedom and choice. The shamans wish to remind us is that Jesus wasn't a Christian, and Buddha wasn't a Buddhist. This means that we can certainly honor and learn from these great examples of who we are when we fully uncover our true nature. Nonetheless, we can follow our own footsteps and find our own direct connection to the Source and joy that is life. I always like to refer to the words of Jesus when he said, "You are all sons of God...these things and greater you shall do."

So, in the meantime, I honor and appreciate all of the beautiful and serving aspects of the world's religions, and what they do for so many people by way of charity, comfort, soothing, community, celebration, and worship in order to help people to feel better and align with their desires, and thus allow them to manifest (Rule of Receptivity). At the same time, I am aware of how religion is sometimes used to suppress, and to create or perpetuate fear, just like other institutions that involve people who sometimes have a personal agenda based on their own fear and self-righteousness.

I use this awareness only to help those who are looking for ways to heal or find better solutions for their lives, and to find more clear and pure connections to their religion, faith, or spirituality. Essentially, my goal as a shaman, and the core goal of the religions, is the same. We do not have to reject or stop practicing our religions to make use of this Shamanic perspective; but we can make them alive, interactive, and participatory once again. We can deepen our faith and understanding, and broaden the practical knowledge they bring to our lives. We can honor all of the teachings, see the commonality at the core of each one, and allow them to evolve with us. We can learn that God still speaks to us in all forms, not just from pages that were written thousands of years ago.

When the Spanish Conquistadors first came to Peru and approached the leader of the Inka empire with their version of the Bible saying, "This is the word of God," the Inka leader put the book to his ear and listened for a while. He then threw the book to the ground saying, "What kind of God is this that does not speak?!" This of course was a big mistake, as the Conquistadors promptly tied him to four horses and quartered him for desecrating the Holy Book. The Conquistadors were so enmeshed in their myths that they preferred to kill those that challenged them, rather than entertain the possibility that there was room for more than one truth. Our myths do not just come from our religions either; we are capable of imprisoning ourselves in the stories that we have created on our own as well. All too often, I see people who have rejected the religion they were raised with only to adopt another or create their own with their own set of limiting beliefs and hierarchy. They are still giving their power away, whether it is to a guru or a scientist, or some other "higher" authority outside of themselves.

Of mythology and reality, Joseph Campbell said, "Reality is those mythologies we have not yet seen through." Concerning the sort of unconscious life contracts we get ourselves into as the Mythic informs the Psycho-spiritual, he also said, "If you don't learn it, you marry it." This is true not only for our spouses, but also for our careers, health conditions, and so on. So it is not that we need to reject or forget our mythologies altogether, we just need to become conscious of how they may be influencing our lives and adjust them to match the lives we prefer to experience. The shamans tell us that we were never really kicked out of the Garden, and that we don't need to have an antagonistic relationship with Nature. They say that there is no independent source of darkness or evil, nor is there a judging God, except in the hearts and minds of humans. So there is no need to engage in battles, but instead we can engage in the healing journey of our hearts and minds today. Having seen through those mythologies, we can create a reality that reflects our true nature of harmony, love, compassion, and joy.

The reason that the old religions are becoming more and more contentious within our minds, is that the evolution of human consciousness, education, and understanding takes power away from the old stories as they become harder to believe, and less useful. For instance, people once had faith in, or believed that, the earth was flat, and today it would be quite difficult for someone to believe that the earth is flat. A religious worldview and practice based on a scientifically plausible set of stories would stand a much better chance of serving its followers and surviving without contention. This still leaves room for many different religions and practices, and at the same time allows for a harmonious marriage with science.

Faith is not accepting blindly, without any kind of evidence, someone else's worldview even if he claims it came from God. My faith lies firmly rooted in the notion that regardless of my religious or scientific associations, I have the equal opportunity of receiving what I ask for, just as the sun will always shine on me, and gravity will always work for me here on the earth. Religions have formed around extraordinary beings, and sciences have formed around geniuses, but these stories are not something beyond our reach. Rather, they offer us formulas and examples of how we can get the most joy with the least amount of fear and powerlessness while we are here.

Let's shift to what we can appreciate about the current religions and sciences. Certainly many religions and spiritual practices around the world have offered tremendous service in bringing together communities and fostering a sense of belonging, value, contribution, passion, and purpose. Likewise, they have contributed greatly to the improvement of quality of life in terms of education, healthcare, art, and compassion. They hold the core Universal truths, and inspire individuals and groups to dream and pray a better world into being. The sciences have brought us greater understanding of all matters of the Universe and certainly many more ways to enjoy life on earth through technological innovations. Both religion and science have brought invaluable tools for expanding the creative process in this infinite sandbox we call the earth and Universe. Religion has enriched our lives with many beautiful myths, parables, lessons, and guidelines; and science has helped us to see both deeper into the previously invisible spaces. In addition, both have expanded the mystery and awe of the process and creation of the Universe as they often raise more questions than they answer.

Vision for Spirituality and Materialism
The core of the vision for spirituality and materialism is to recognize that they can function together to promote further understanding of life and the Universe, thus promoting deep healing and great joy. Science can broaden to support the efficacy of spiritual and non-physical approaches to healing and evolution of consciousness. Spirituality can lighten up and focus on improving the quality of life now on the Earth, as opposed to later in Heaven or some other transcendent location, as well as the quality of life for all subsequent lifetimes and generations here on the Earth. Science can help us to understand that prayer has a statistically significant impact on cure rates for diseases and crime rates in neighborhoods for example. Spirituality can help us to embrace the diversity and messiness of the biological aspects of Creation, and to re-animate matter.

In this vision, a diverse set of religious practices and organizations focus on empowering and serving their followers, encouraging each to be a follower of his/her own heart, while at the same time allowing all other approaches without contention. And if a religion begins to lose its following, it will allow change, or scale down, and even cease to exist as an organization, thus allowing the free choice and evolution of the human spirit to continue. In this way, the most sustainable and useful approaches for humanity, the planet, and the Universe will thrive and grow. Furthermore, in the vision, people from diverse spiritual and scientific backgrounds will freely and openly exchange ideas, philosophies, and approaches, along with the evidence of their effectiveness. Hierarchy flattens into an egalitarian sandbox, allowing people to share ideas, and to honor all participants equally.

Notes on Your Vision for Spirituality and Materialism:

Chapter 9
Justice and Law

True justice serves to heal and reduce harm and create greater welfare, as in the Sanskrit root *yos*, which translates to mean "welfare." Ironically, what we call justice today, and what is widely practiced as such in the modern world, often does more harm than healing. Our justice system is based on the concept of an eye for an eye, and uses fear as its main weapon in the war on crime. True reform, restoration, and healing are rare, because of how most modern cultures address the behavior of people who are fearful, confused, and/or truly ill and acting out as a result. Sometimes these crimes appear to be committed by cool and conniving people that, in our view, must be inherently bad—or in the extreme, influenced by an evil force. Most of the time, however, it is obvious that crimes are committed as an act of desperation based on the core state of fear. For example, a person steals money in order to feed an addiction, or to simply feed him or herself. Or a person kills another for fear that the other is, or will be, taking something from them, whether this something is a possession or peace of mind. A rape might occur because a person fears that they have no power, or that they will never be offered physical pleasure consensually. Corporate or Government injustices also tend to be related to this drive for power over others, which is based on the fear that "I am either going to get screwed, or I am going to be the screwer; or in my control over others, I can make sure that nobody gets screwed." Our current justice system tends to increase these underlying fears and desperation. Or, at best, it goes after only the outward Psycho-spiritual symptoms, and thus backfires on its own goal.

Based on what we know about the Rule of Resonance and Receptivity, can we continue to assume that a person can assert himself into our experience, thus presenting an exception to these rules? The belief that another can force himself into our reality, by hurting us or stealing from us, is another example of the victim/perpetrator/rescuer mentality that we discussed earlier. Further, can we continue to assume that we are capable of passing judgment as to the reasons for, and consequences of, any one act? These are difficult questions for people of the precept - or law driven people - to answer, let alone ask. When we are in that fear-based victim consciousness, it seems completely reasonable to fight for justice until every person with an ounce of injustice in their bones is dead, behind bars, or rehabilitated. But over the long term, the current system of precepts, judgments, and punishment has proven ineffective and even detrimental to living in harmony, relative safety, and well-being. Our jails and prisons continue to fill beyond capacity, and the number and severity of crimes continue to rise. This is because short of the most severe torture, the fear of punishment fails to surpass the fear of living in an increasingly judgmental, righteous, competitive, and disenfranchising world. This is also why studies show that the likelihood of being caught - and thereby judged - is a greater deterrent to crime than the severity of punishment. Escalation of forces, weaponry, and punishment makes it worse, and creates more battles in the neighborhoods, battles with "rogue states," and battles with and between global crime rings, governments, and corporations. This is simply because these methods escalate the fear-based power of righteous judgment. For example, if I have bigger guns or more money, I must be more right, and you must be more wrong. And when do the battles end? Is it when we all agree with the worldview of one man or woman, or a consensus of a majority that can assert its physical and psychological influence on the minority? And who appoints that ultimate judge? The truth is that under the current scenario, the battles never end unless and until there is one person left standing. As Gandhi put it, if we continue an eye for an eye, eventually we will all be blind.

Clearly, most of those involved in the current justice systems believe that they are making the world a better place; and shamans share that desire to make the world a better place. Given the real opportunity for an abundant, allowing, and honoring world, where diversity is truly honored, most "criminals" would also share that goal on the deepest levels. Certainly there may be benefit, under the current conditions, to removing some of the criminals from society temporarily, if for no other reason than to give them time to heal and to protect them. This is assuming, of course, that that we offer true healing within our current system. The problem is that the conditions and management of the majority of the prison system frequently creates even more wounding and reason for more criminal behavior. However, some existing prison programs truly help to heal criminals, and improve the overall system. For example, I know of several Native American teachers and healers who conduct Sweat Lodge cleansing, teaching, and praying ceremonies within prisons. My great friend and benefactor Dean Hillyer, also frequents prisons, teaching much of the concepts presented in this book.

Vision for Justice and Law
In restorative justice systems, the community, the "criminal," and the "victim" come together in a circle to openly dialogue. The process helps everyone to understand and address the true cause of the act, and to come up with a constructive way to make amends,

heal, and avoid repeating the offense. In these systems, the probability of repeat offenses is much lower than in punitive justice systems; and, the probability that the "criminal" becomes a contributing and harmonious part of the community is much higher than in any punitive justice system. Restorative justice systems are more common amongst indigenous cultures. This offers the possibility for the entire community to heal and to improve the quality of life for all of its members.

Some would argue that restorative justice works fine in a simple village setting, but that in today's modern and complex world it will be too difficult. They say that too many people have just fallen through the cracks, and the only solution is to remove them from society, and that at this point there is no way to heal or restore most of these completely lost souls. I agree that the current situation has a lot of momentum behind it. There are souls that are so wounded and fearful, with the subsequent Psycho-spiritual and physical imbalances, that we need the current system as an acute intervention and starting point. However, as in our discussion about education, one size does not fit all. We need to address all layers of the problem with varying degrees of intervention. True justice will be much easier to achieve if we first implement much of our vision from the previous sections of this book.

We can expand upon the restorative justice model with the principles and healing techniques presented in this book, and move to an integral model of justice based on true healing, understanding, allowing, love, and compassion. Over time, the need to take acute actions to protect those who write the scripts from those who are acting in them will gradually decline. This will lead to a greater allowing and freedom, based on appreciation and encouragement in place of fear and punishment, which will in turn lead to increased harmony, peace, and abundance for all who choose it. We will begin a fundamental shift toward allowing and encouraging participation in society based on each person's inclination toward how she can contribute and express her gifts. Thus, each individual will feel like a valuable and appreciated part of society, and will be able to stay in the state of love and connection to Source. This paradigm shift will start with local communities and spread to nations.

One of my clients is on the forefront of a new integral healing approach to law referred to as Collaborative Law. Instead of the traditional situation where two opposing lawyers battle to the end, say for example in a divorce case, in Collaborative Law, a team is gathered that includes a healing professional such as a psychologist, relationship counselor, or shaman along with the lawyers and clients. While the road may still be rough due to the raw feelings from the relationship ending, the result of this collaborative approach allows for greater healing and amicable relationships for the clients going forward. What was once mostly a win-lose proposition now becomes a win-win solution.

Notes on Your Vision for Justice and Law:

Chapter 10
Government and Politics

The vast majority of modern cultures today are comprised of people of the precept. In these cultures, lawmakers, lawyers, and enforcers dominate government and politics. At this point in the book, the shortcomings of such an approach should be clear. Today's modern governments and political systems, including "democratic," oligarchic, monarchic, benevolent and malevolent dictatorships, socialistic, sectarian, and communistic systems to name a few, share many of the burdens of our old paradigm: judgment, righteousness, fear, and battle.

The reason I put democratic in quotes is that there are very few purely democratic systems in the world. A pure democracy depends on the education and participation of the entire population. The people vote directly on every issue, and the majority determines the actions to be taken. In the United States, we do not have a pure democracy, but rather a Republic. A relatively small part of the population votes for individual representatives to become the lawmakers and decision makers. Once they are voted into office, they are not completely beholden to the majority of their constituents for their decisions, and in some cases may become more beholden to those willing to pay them the most money, the so-called "special interests." Critics would say that some of the representatives are more concerned with their own judgments, or at worst their next campaign funding and favors. Thus, large corporations and the wealthiest have a greater influence over those representatives. While there are checks and balances built into the system, some have characterized it as more of an oligarchy.

In an oligarchy, the general population tends to feel increasingly powerless and disenfranchised, and tends to become more apathetic and less willing to put in the energy to educate themselves and encourage their neighbors to do the same. This apathy serves to perpetuate the licenses and power of the more exclusive representatives, along with their very real influences. Moreover, since for the majority of the people things don't seem quite bad enough to cause a revolution, they would prefer not to hear about it—and certainly not such a cynical view as I have just presented. At the same time, those who do have the strong desire to change things and become activists are generally pushing so hard against the established political system that, based on the rules of the Universe, they are inadvertently attracting more of the same. Note that these activists are often labeled as unpatriotic, criminals, or traitors, and may end up literally imprisoned or killed for their words and actions.

People want to believe that this government is a real democracy, that all representatives have their best interests in mind, and that the government and representatives must be intelligent and benevolent enough to do the right thing. Perhaps the U.S. style of democracy has created the best opportunities for materialistic gain and in some measures, the best quality of life ever experienced by at least some portion of the population. In reality, recent research shows that Denmark's social system of government offers the best overall quality of life in measures such as overall health, crime rates, education, equality, sustainability, and so on. Relative to a suppressive malevolent dictatorship, statistical measures of quality of life would of course favor both the U.S. and Danish systems for example. However, depending on who conducts the surveys and what decides true quality of life, the statistics relative to some of the other systems throughout history might have shown even better ways to govern or not govern at all, for example ancient Greece, the pre-Columbian Americas, the Pacific Islands, Ancient China and India, and so on.

In this increasingly global world and economy, there seems to be a movement towards a one-world government and political system modeled after the relatively new experiment of the United States of America. The problem with this approach is in deciding on what this one system will be, how do we determine which one truly is the best. Further, how do we maintain and honor the diversity that makes it fun to come to the Earth in the first place and that was the original spirit of the founding of the U.S.? It seems that a homogenous world system goes against the principles of Creation and nature's apparent quest for greater diversity and complexity. For this reason, there may always be a fundamental undercurrent of resistance to anything that attempts to take away freedom to choose and to be one's original authentic self.

It is really a moot point to analyze and determine which system would serve best under the new paradigm of creator consciousness, just as it would be moot to argue which system would have worked best when the only humans on the planet were dwelling in caves. And of course, going back in time is never a viable solution in an ever-expanding Creation and consciousness, so cave dwelling is not the answer either. Government and political systems, whether working or not and whether pure or corrupt, are just manifestations of the collective asking that has arisen from the masculine warrior myths. And each individual in that collective will only experience what she is asking for, even from within the collective manifestation. The truth is that people, corporations, institutions, and governments have no power over your own experience, and only seem to if you choose to give this power to them.

Some visionaries express the virtues of total anarchy, meaning no government and no man-made laws, with each person tending to their own asking and receiving in harmony with their community. And from the purely natural and broadest perspective, this approach has its merits. The problem is that it is not a very graceful solution under the current circumstances. It would be like flinging open the doors of the insane asylum before healing the insane, or even educating them on how to live outside of the walls. Eventually, after much messiness, things would settle down and some levels of decentralized care and self-governing would form within cooperative communities, much like in primitive villages. But this would be going backwards in the creative evolutionary process and may not be the ultimate solution for the world today, unless we are forced back there by some huge calamity or rebalancing. In times of great contrast, going back to simpler times is quite seductive, but would be wholly unfulfilling to a creature that thrives on expansion and creating new realities. That creature then might start the process all over again, and we would be back where we are now.

As long as there is diversity and drama in the creative process, there will be naturally forming governing and political bodies of some kind. There will always be visionaries who see what is possible, and experts who understand more than anyone else does. People will tend to follow these natural leaders and make choices about whom they follow. This means there will be people expressing their opinions about their choices, and others who will be influenced, and so on. Politics and government is a natural phenomenon of creation. Perhaps at least people of power and knowledge—people who are being influenced and influencing— will not experience politics or a government that is manipulative and abusive, but instead one which truly serves the whole.

Vision for Government and Politics

Current systems of government and politics remain as diverse as the people they serve. As more people heal and come into their power as Creators, systems that do not naturally serve will disappear with grace and ease. The new paradigm of creator consciousness leads to people who understand the rules of resonance, receptivity, and allowing. As we collectively shift to the new paradigm, those who find joy in making a living as lawyers and politicians will increasingly find their joy in other ways as the need for those skills become less common. In the meantime, those in law and politics, and the government systems they serve, will heal to the extent that they create positive change from within the system. All institutions, from local neighborhoods to global ones, will focus their mission on empowering people, healing, and allowing more freedom and diversity, including the freedom of any person to choose contrasting experiences like pain and bondage. These institutions, systems of government, and politics will be driven by the fullness of life and the full expression of the people they serve in a holistic and truly sustainable fashion. They will manage, transform, and distribute resources in such a way that honors the balance necessary to sustain all life on the planet.

Notes on Your Vision for Government and Politics:

Chapter 11
Environment and Resources

At no other time in history has the general public known more about the human impact on the ecosystem of the earth than they do today; and at no other known time in history has that impact been greater than it is now. Awareness and fear about the sustainability of our species and many other species is growing along with the seriousness of the reality of the situation. From the perspective of the universal rules, we know that awareness of the problem or contrasting experience is the first step. Ideally, awareness is followed by the second step, which is to focus on what is working and what we would prefer the reality to be.

A mountain of scientific evidence suggests that given the current amount of known resources, and given the current technologies for extracting and using them, the earth can only sustain a population of about two billion humans... and this is only if we are all riding bicycles to work. With the current population approaching eight billion humans, there is a significant imbalance in the ecosystem that many prognosticators and prophecies believe will resolve itself relatively soon through the elimination of about two-thirds of the human population. There are numerous ways in which this rebalancing can manifest including drought, flooding, disease, and tremendous natural disasters, including those resulting from global warming, pollution, and wars. Evidence of these mechanisms is already upon us as I write this book.

Perhaps there is already to much momentum behind the current reality and its apparent resolution, but it is definitely worth looking at, calling in, and dreaming into being the alternatives, if not for the current eight billion of us at this point in time, then at least for whatever number remain in physical form going forward. Likewise, in the true spirit of dreaming your world into being, I believe miracles can occur that are beyond our wildest imagination, and would allow for completely unpredictable and elegant resolutions to the issues facing our environment and resources.

If we focus on the transformation of our relationship to the environment through external technologies alone, we may only prolong the inevitable rebalancing. Likewise, if resource and consumption intensive economies continue to spread, which seem to require infinite growth to sustain themselves, even if the growth is "green", it appears that a rebalancing may have to occur at some point. As populations in places like China, India, South America, and Africa seek to follow the industrial experiences common to Europe and North America, consumption of resources may rise exponentially, thus accelerating and deepening the imbalances. Moreover, since it seems completely unreasonable to stem or reverse human/Creator nature to seek greater complexity, it seems unlikely that a voluntary reduction of resource use is achievable anytime soon.

Switching to renewable, reusable resource use seems like the best alternative under these circumstances; however, we don't fully understand the potential impact of these alternative technologies and the impact of more and more people using them. For example, if everyone had a solar panel or wind turbine in her home, there may be a global impact from absorbing and transforming that energy to run our appliances, for example, as opposed to it just being absorbed by plants and so on. We can use more nuclear energy, which while relatively clean compared to coal and oil, still generates a tremendous amount of heat as a by-product. And in the extreme, even if we came up with a perpetual motion machine or cars that run on "free" energy, would it still be okay if all eight billion people owned one or more of these cars? Where would we park them, and what kind of surface would we drive them on? The bottom line is that, regardless of the technology, there will likely be an impact on the environment and resources.

This leads me back to the inner technologies. What I mean by inner technologies is living by the notion of "ask and it is given" by focusing on the ideal experiences (with regard to the use of our resources and the environment) that we would like now and going forward. "Ask and it is given" is either always true or never true, and I personally have enough evidence and knowledge to believe it is true without exception. So let us say I am one of any number of people on the planet living in one of the myriad of possible conditions and environments, and I decide that I would like a new experience, say more food, or new transportation, or a new residence, anything for any reason. Given the rules of the Universe, I start by imagining what the experience will feel like, and I include in the asking process the sustainability of this experience for me and all other entities on the Earth, and even in the known Universe, such that my experience will lead to only better and more positive experiences for me and all-that-is. If enough people hold a similar vision, the question becomes how will Source make this happen on a seemingly resource limited Earth? I don't know how to answer that question, and at this point, you may be thinking I'm completely unrealistic. But why not continue to give this "ask and it is given" scenario a chance since we may be pleasantly surprised by how the manifestation unfolds.

If the experiences we truly desire are fulfilling enough without the need to consume more resources, then this might be one answer. If we could freely express and receive our natural gifts through our work, then we may not need to fill the void as much with more stuff. Some say the resource and consumption intensive economies drive the need to constantly produce more material goods for ever-increasing profits, and therefore encourage more consumption; and this is all kept running by increasingly unfulfilled workers in a vicious cycle. If more and more people are finding their most enjoyable and fulfilling work, there may be hope for dreaming a life into being that balances personal fulfillment with a truly sustainable environment and use of resources.

Vision for Environment and Resources

My vision for a sustainable environment and use of resources encourages all-that-is to thrive more than ever before. It involves a combination of using alternative external technologies along with the full understanding and practicing of the rules of the Universe (inner technologies) in the short term; and, by coming to an education and business system that provides greater fulfillment and expression for the individual for long term balance and sustainability. Until we obtain more mastery over creating our reality, including resource use and the environment, more people will be caretakers of the Earth, which includes their own bodies. As more people make choices that support a more sustainable and balanced life, the larger organizations will follow suit by producing and offering the best alternatives for maximizing positive impacts on the environment, while allowing humans to pursue more complexity and greater levels of experience and fulfillment.

Global cooperation in the pursuit and use of the best external technologies improves the quality of the environment for the benefit of all life everywhere, while offering more opportunities for the population to align internally with vibrational choices that create the preferred individual experiences as well as the collective experiences of all life on Earth and in the Universe.

Notes on Your Vision for Environment and Resources:

Chapter 12
Business and Economy

There have been, and continue to be, many alternative approaches to business and economy across the globe. Increasingly, the majority of human populations are adopting resource and consumption intensive systems. The masculine warrior mythologies of the modern Western world form the basis of many of these systems. These mythologies are essentially based on the notion that Creation is finished and limited; and therefore, those seeking to feel more secure may be compelled to gain control over as much of the limited amount of resources as they feel is necessary. Gaining some control over the external circumstance that appear to dictate his or her experience gives a person the illusion of security and power, but is just another part of the victim/perpetrator/rescuer consciousness. It makes it seem as though the rules of the Universe can be defied, like defying gravity. It may seem plausible for a relatively short period of time, but "ask and it is given" always prevails, and regardless of the efforts to hoard and protect resources, and control external circumstances, the person's internal experiences cannot be avoided. One cannot escape the ultimate responsibility inherent in being the creator of one's own experiences, without exception.

It may be obvious by now that both the mythological assumptions, as well as, the definition of quality of life under the resource and consumption intensive systems are flawed in some way. The result of these systems based on ever increasing accumulation of resources may ultimately be summed up by the prophetic line in the Bible, "The meek shall inherit the Earth." The reason this may be true is that ultimately nobody wins the battles for limited resources; and even if one person remains standing with all the resources and control, what quality of life does he or she have left if surrounded by those who have lost out? A certain amount of philanthropy helps to bring balance to this approach, but it seems to be a somewhat inefficient and insufficient way of ensuring that resources are doled out evenly enough to maintain stability and harmony. I am not advocating limiting anyone's desire to have more, but I am recognizing as I proposed in the previous section, that a healthy and fulfilled individual's desires may be less oriented to having more stuff, and instead towards having more relational experiences.

Some would argue that eliminating the competition-based economies would thwart technological innovation and expansion of increased quality of life available to those who have the ambition to pursue such innovation; and this may even be true to some extent, but what are the flawed assumptions of this argument? One may be that technological innovation is the answer to the world's problems, and there is plenty of evidence to the contrary where "solutions" end up causing more and bigger problems. Second is the notion that all humans have the same values and ambitions, as well as a level playing field to engage in the competition, neither of which seems to be true. The third assumption is that innovation is driven only by competition. Innovation can also be driven by our curious and creative nature, simply for the joy of it.

There are successful economic systems based on cooperation and responsibility informed by the reality of "ask and it is given." These can be found in the tribal cultures that have not been influenced by the West. The Q'ero of Peru, for example, have a saying, "For you today, for me tomorrow," where one family will spend today helping to build a house or tend the harvest for another family, and tomorrow the favor will be returned. They don't even have the need for a proxy-based or fiat monetary system. There is never a need to hoard for fear of a day when "ask and it is given" might not work. And if resources are stored, it is for the benefit of the entire community, in case of times of difficulty.

What we can appreciate about the current economic and business systems is that they do provide a means for rapid acceleration of increased opportunities for increasingly diverse experiences on the planet. Essentially, we can get more and get it faster—including the side effects and the contrast. This has also produced greater desire in general as we witness others having more experiences. We could even argue this has been a catalyst for our evolution.

Vision for Business and Economy
As people progress in their healing processes and step beyond the core fear inherent in the current dominant mythologies, they will naturally be inspired to make resources available to those who want them. Businesses will serve the community and encourage those who choose to participate in a cooperative and nurturing way. Participants within these systems will be educated and encouraged to find and express their greatest, most fulfilling, and most joyful gifts. Economies will move from the purpose of expansion and innovation to the purpose of joy, cooperation, and harmony where expansion and innovation are possible byproducts.

What if a supervisor sat down with each member of a work group and told them they would be evaluated and rewarded based on the amount of help they offered to their co-workers, as opposed to how much more productive they could be relative to their co-workers? Therefore, each worker came to work looking for opportunities to help her fellow workers succeed. Would productivity and quality of the work experience improve relative to a competitive, cutthroat, work environment where it is each person for herself? I believe this alone would create a radical improvement over the majority of work environments we see today, and have grown used to over recent decades. In the recently published, best selling business book "Influencer: The Power to Change Anything," one of the key ways suggested to create a positive influence in a group is to start by being the one who truly cares and advocates for the success of each of the other members of the group. My vision is that every worker has the opportunity to support and cooperate with each other from the place of the influencer such that this new paradigm of cooperation spreads from the smallest unit up to the entire global business and economic system.

Notes on Your Vision for Business and Economy:

Chapter 13
Arts and Media

One of the many things that I admire about my teacher Alberto is that he walks his talk by remaining open and growing in his art. I've heard him say on several occasions that his deepest calling is as a poet. When presented with materials that focus on using the mind to manifest, he always points out that it is missing the heart, the love. This has been a great lesson for me personally, as I recognize that life is more about the art and poetry that moves us, the true and beautiful drama, more than logic, reasoning, accuracy, and efficiency. Really, the greatest accomplishments through history have come from inspiration or serendipity, whether it is a Leonardo Da Vinci or Helen Keller, or inward journeys beyond the confines of normal states of consciousness by the shamans and modern researchers like Stan Grof and Timothy Leary. To make art and the expression of art through media anything less than one of the most important aspects of life, is to deny life itself. In our modern world dominated by the logic and reasoning of the brain, and the resulting lifelessness, it is no wonder that drugs and all other forms of getting out of the brain and into the body have become an epidemic. We are all desperately searching for the lost art of life.

Somehow, art and media have become scapegoats for the very problems that suppression of art and media has created. Therefore, we have been in a vicious cycle of cutting the arts out of schools and using media only to perpetuate the limiting fear-based myths. Throughout history, we have looked back and given names to these periods of expansion and suppression of free artistic expression. We call times of suppression "Dark Ages" and times of free expression "Renaissance." Yet we don't seem to learn from history, and because of our Energetic wounds and myths, we tend to repeat the same patterns and cycles. I think that when we look back on this period of the last five centuries, we will designate it as another Dark Age. An age when the masculine dominated logic and reasoning took over and attempted to squeeze the last drop of life blood out of our human bodies, and kept our minds functioning like laptop computers, or more like shoulder-top computers. The great thing about life and biology, however, is that it always finds a way to survive and ultimately thrive—the jungle will always reclaim the city, and the body always wins over the mind, even it if has to wait until the final last word, or the final breath to do so.

This ultimate significance of art over logic is even recognized by the leaders of our greatest armies. In the book "Blink: The Power of Thinking without Thinking" by Malcolm Gladwell, military strategists acknowledge through experimentation that battles are won by decisions based on gut instincts and actions, over the more logical and reasonable choices. The greatest and most successful business leaders have acknowledged this as well. Art, poetry, beauty, and "mu shin" or no mind, are the greatest secrets to success, thriving, joy, and love, no matter how you look at it and how you measure it.

Vision for Art and Media
Emphasis and resources are given to encourage free artistic expression from early education and into all aspects of life, most notably all forms of architecture, design, performing arts, music, and all artistic media. The profit motive takes a back seat, if any seat at all, to artistic expression, beauty, and feelings. Media in

particular is supported and encouraged to play an uncensored role in the art, poetry, and drama of the creative life process.

I will use an example of the architectural design and land use work that I engage in with my friend and colleague Vladimir Frank. Together we have combined the alive Energetic aspects of the building space, the land, the landscaping, and the placement and sacred geometries from the Shamanic wisdom and techniques; and joined these with Vladimir's natural heart, soul, compassion, artistic beauty, and technical expertise that have always been in his work. One such project completed in early 2008 for new guest units at the Post Ranch Inn has received accolades from all those who have experienced this powerful combination. Guests who stay in these new units are positively affected on all layers of their being.

To summarize the vision for art and media, but also a fitting way to conclude this book, as it is applicable to many of the subjects of our vision, the mission statement of Vladimir's architectural firm reads:

> Vladimir's dedication to quality in design, environmental responsibility and commitment to sustainable architecture has always been the guiding principle of his work. More than just being environmentally friendly, his architecture strives to enhance and amplify the experience of nature by the seamless approach between the interior and exterior environment.
>
> Vladimir practices active architecture that integrates the human context of cultural, social, emotional, psychological, and physical needs to create an

environment, which elevates and inspires human potential. In the last several years, his projects have been inspired by the ancient wisdom of sacred geometry. This knowledge is offering unique approaches to architectural solutions.

This approach to architecture and design when applied to the facilities that house our families, schools, government, businesses, scientific research facilities, and our places of art, healing and prayer, serves as a great model for our potential when we take the holistic Shamanic approach. In this way, the architect's work and the shaman's work are the same, to inspire creativity, freedom, power, and joy.

Notes on Your Vision for Arts and Media:

Appendix A
Practical and Powerful Meditation Techniques

The following is a list of my favorite meditation practices from over the years, and what I currently teach my clients, who are mostly high-achieving Westerners, and who wouldn't take the time to do a full-blown Eastern meditation practice if their life depended on it. Most of these techniques can be practiced anywhere at anytime, with no special preparation required. As true practices, the beauty of these techniques is that after a while you will no longer need to practice, and the awareness, focus, and abilities you attain will be available to you all of the time. Just like learning a musical instrument, once you get it, you just jam; you don't need to practice anymore. You may want to try each of them, and see which you enjoy doing the most, and which seems to be most effective for you. Just as with the musical instrument, if you want to play the piano, and someone hands you a guitar, you are not likely to continue to practice. Enjoyment is key.

1.   The first practice helps you to achieve awareness of your body, so that you can recognize when you are holding tension, and let it go by purposely creating contrast. This one is excellent to do while lying in bed, at the end of the day.
   • Be in any comfortable position; take three deep breaths feeling the air course through your body. Close your eyes for the rest of the meditation.
   • Place your attention first on your feet and gently tense or squeeze the muscles of your feet, then release. Notice how each state feels. Notice the contrast. Do this squeezing and releasing three times for each major muscle group all the way

up your body: feet, calves, thighs, buttocks, stomach, back, chest, arms, shoulders, neck and head.

- Scan back through your body starting at the feet, just to notice if you are still holding tension in any part of your body, and release it. Remember to breathe.
- The more you practice this the more you will be aware of your body, and where it might be tense, and you will be able to release it. If you fall asleep, that's good too; you probably need the rest more than anything else at the moment, for without enough energy, there is very little of anything that we can do.

2. This next meditation is wonderful for relaxing and broadening our perspective, so that we are not caught up as much in the various contrasting experiences and dramas of our lives.

- Start with the three deep breaths and scanning your body for any places that you can let go.
- Allow your consciousness to drop down from behind your eyes, to behind your mouth, as if you are looking out through your mouth, then your throat, then and your chest from behind your heart, where you see your heart in front of you beating. Imagine seeing the heart and the lungs expanding and contracting on either side.
- Enter into your heart, and see it pumping the blood all around you as the muscles rhythmically contract, and the valves open and close. In the center of your heart, see a small sphere of bluish golden and white light; enter that sphere of light, which is the center of your luminous body, and is outside of the confines of ordinary space and time.
- Merge with the light as if you are anywhere along its edge, looking into the space held within the sphere.

- With each inhalation, allow the sphere to expand, first surrounding your heart, then your chest, then your whole body, then the room, then the building, the city, the state, the country, the continent, and the whole earth. You can keep going to the solar system, the galaxy and out to the edge of the Universe if you wish.
- Whenever you want, reverse the expansion, and bring your consciousness and the sphere of light back around each space, until you are back inside your heart.
- Step out of the sphere of light into your heart, seeing the blood moving and carrying the nutrients and oxygen, even better than before.
- Back your way out of the heart, return up to behind your eyes, and open your eyes.

3. This next technique is somewhat similar in nature to the first, and can be added to the end of it as well. It's good for cleansing and for strengthening your connection to your Source of energy and to the Earth that takes our wastes/combusted energy and recycles it. Both are very important connections for maintaining your energy and your feelings of support and nurturing.

- Be in any comfortable position; take three deep breaths feeling the air course through your body. Close your eyes for the rest of the meditation.
- Now, as you inhale see a column of light coming in to the top of your head, and see the light going to every cell of your body. The column of light can originate in space, from the world of the non-physical Source, or from the Sun.
- As you exhale, see a column of light going out the bottom of your body/torso (your perineum) into the Earth. This light

contains any wastes from your cells that the new light that is
coming in has cleansed.

- Do this for as long as you like. You may have noticed
  when you do these visualizations, you are not thinking of
  anything else – that's meditation, focusing on only one thing.

4. Another good meditation for focus and awareness can be done
while walking. There is a variation for whether you are walking to
get somewhere or just walking for the purpose of this meditation.

- If just for the purpose of meditation, as you slowly take
  each step, feel the ground under your feet, noticing every
  variation in pressure and balance.
- If you are going somewhere, coordinate your breathing
  with your steps; for example, inhale for three steps, exhale for
  three steps. Any meditation with breath as a focus is powerful.

5. This technique is borrowed from Eastern sources that is related
to breath, and makes use of the vibration of words, in this case
Sanskrit, where both the meaning and the vibration are beneficial.
Also, this meditation can be done at any time and anywhere since
your eyes can be open.

- Be in any comfortable position; take three deep breaths
  feeling the air course through your body. Close your eyes for
  part of the meditation and open them for part to feel the
  difference.
- From now until you feel finished, as you inhale say to
  yourself silently the word "Hahm," and as you exhale, say to
  yourself silently the word "Sah."
- Essentially what you are saying in meaning is "I am that."
  This is similar to the Native American concept and way of
  relating to the external world by saying for example "that tree

in me, that mountain in me, that person in me," so that there is a constant unity consciousness. The lack of separateness helps relax us, and reduce anxiety.

•   Try the meditation using your own language for "I am" on the inhalations and "that" on the exhalations, and notice any difference from the Sanskrit. Most of my clients notice that the Sanskrit is more effective, because the language was created with the vibratory nature of the words in mind.

6. This next set of practices is amazing for developing awareness and for focusing on the moment of now.

•   Wherever you are, close your eyes and listen to every sound that is available to you. Search with your ears for even the subtlest sounds.

•   Next, open your eyes, and notice every color, shade, and texture that is available for you to see.

•   Then close your eyes again and feel every feeling available; for example, temperature variation on your skin, the air passing through your nose and into your lungs, your heartbeat, the pressure of your feet on the ground, or of your body on the seat or ground.

•   Now, with your eyes closed, see the sounds [see them as sound waves, not the object making the sound]. Then open your eyes, and hear the colors or feel the colors. This is called Synesthesia. Being able to actually do this is not the goal. Instead, it is in the act of attempting it that you are totally focused, and training your mind in awareness. This can also lead to an altered state of consciousness that could give you tremendous insights.

•   Another variation of this practice is to attempt to take in all that is available to every sense at the same time.

7. When we are in a room with another person or people, we send out "feelers" or cords from our energy body, usually from around our solar plexus, to connect with them, just like we connect with them through the physical senses of our eyes, ears, and skin (which are all just energy transducers as well). This can also happen over the phone or just thinking of the person. This aspect of engaging is how we can intuit how they are feeling, and empathize with them, or even psychically pick up on their thoughts. This can be very helpful in many ways, whether it is with a friend, family member, or client that we are helping to heal, or in a business meeting or sales call. The problem arises in that we are usually unconscious of making this Energetic connection, and therefore often fail to disengage or draw back the cord when we are no longer "with" that person or group of people. We have not been taught how to disengage. The result is that, through both time and space, we are wasting energy maintaining this connection through which neither you, nor the other party benefits. Enough of these accumulated Energetic cords can cause chronic fatigue, failure to be able to let go of an emotionally charged situation, and/or tons of unwanted thoughts, which are often confused as attention deficit disorder. The shamans are taught early on to consciously cut these cords, and will even "meditate" by literally crossing a sword or feather in front of our bodies in order to do it mythically as well. The following practice is helpful in gaining awareness of the cords, how they can serve us, and how to disengage them when they no longer serve.

- Find a nearby tree (can be done with a stone, animal, or person as well, but a tree is best for practice, because our relationship with it is neutral).

- Bring your consciousness from behind your eyes down into the light in your heart first, just as we did in the second technique, and then down to behind your solar plexus, just under the arch of your ribcage.
- Consciously send a column of light from your belly to the tree. See this cord of light forming in front of you.
- Allow your consciousness to travel through the cord to the tree and into the entire tree.
- Feel the roots in the ground, the water coursing up the trunk and out the branches to the leaves through every cell of your tree body.
- Feel the breeze and the sunlight on your leaves, and the process of converting the sun to sugars that feed your tree body.
- Sense all that is going on with this tree.
- You will also have the memories of the tree as it grew from a tiny sapling each day, with the sun wrapping another band of light around your trunk and branches; and of the seasons and people that have come and gone around you. All of it seeming to move with the speed of a hummingbird from your long-term tree perspective.
- When you are ready, return through the energy cord to your body, and feel once again all that is going on in your human body. Feel your breath, the blood coursing through your veins, and the joy of being so highly mobile.
- Now consciously retract the cord back to your body, or dissolve it and see your energy body around you as a smooth egg, retracting or dissolving any other cords that may be out there. The only cords that remain are into the top of your head from your Source, and out of the bottom of your torso to the Earth, so that you look like a pearl on a string.

- Retract or dissolve any cord in the same way, anytime you find yourself thinking of a person or past or future event that you don't need to be engaged in at the moment, or anytime you are having trouble focusing your thoughts, or when you feel inexplicably low in energy.
- You can supplement the mental aspect of this technique with a Literal and Mythic practice such as tracing over your body with a knife, sword, feather, or hands. I use a technique called the "Kahuna Break" that involves rubbing the hands together at solar plexus level, pushing one hand away from the body three times, then using the other hand to cut down in front of the body, and back up to "zip-up" the energy body.

8. This technique is based on the Rule of Receptivity, which means that everything you have ever asked for is on it's way, as long as you are a vibrational match to it – and you know that you are a vibrational match to everything you've ever asked for when you are feeling good in any given moment. So if there are things that you can't help observing, thinking about, or talking about in the moment, based on your current state of perception, that aren't making you feel good, then try this 30 second meditation. I call it the 30-second fantasy, and the goal is to get in, feel good, and get out.

- Close your eyes and imagine that you are somewhere beautiful, and the temperature is perfect, you are perfectly comfortable, and all your senses are experiencing pure pleasure. I use a pristine beach with the most beautiful sand and water that I've ever seen. The temperature is perfect, the sky is beautiful, and I'm drinking my favorite drink that was made the best it has ever been made, and tastes like nectar.

- You may have someone with you that you are laughing with and enjoying exhilarating conversation with.
- Now get out and open your eyes. The idea is to stay in not much more than 30 seconds, just long enough to feel good and before anything or anyone comes along that doesn't feel so good.
- It is helpful to choose a location and person/people that are a total fantasy, so that any old experiences or feelings, whether conscious or unconscious, do not interfere.

9. In conjunction with the 30-second fantasy for allowing, there are several techniques for clearly and deliberately asking for what you desire in the first place; one such method I call "pre-journaling." The first thing to do upon waking in the morning is to go on what Abraham-Hicks calls "A rampage of appreciation" for all that is in your life. Then, acknowledge with gratitude, and get in the feeling place of all that is on it's way, either for that day, for longer time frames, or even shorter segments of time, like your next meeting. You can write it on paper, or in your mind. The idea is to not so much imagine the exact course of events, which you can, but to make sure that you feel the feeling that you want to feel, as the events unfold. And remember to dig to the very core of whatever it is that you desire; for example, do you want a million dollars, or do you want to be able to do whatever you enjoy most, whenever you want to do it? Or, for another example, do you want to own a carpet, or do you really just want warmth and comfort under your feet. To the extent that you can ask for exact details of your manifestation with no feelings of resistance, that is great. But if there is any feeling of resistance, then you are not a vibrational match, and it may be helpful to be more general, and to

allow the Universe to give you the experience that you want in some other form of manifestation.

10. I think this is a great place to add that evidence suggests, and I have heard from the Abraham-Hicks material as well, that our religious practices of worship, contemplation, and singing hymns, for example, can be effective at getting us aligned with our desires and with Source, depending on your approach. This will be obvious to many who have a spiritual or meditative practice, and it will be helpful to be mindful of this purpose as the practices are performed; as opposed to doing it because you will be punished if you don't. The religious and spiritual practices are successful to the extent that they help you to feel good, support your faith in the concept of "ask and it is given," and are directed toward what you want, as opposed to pushing against what you don't want.

11. Abraham-Hicks says that there is no greater mass connection to Source than occurs unintentionally during a sporting event such as a football game. So if you can't make it to church, temple, mosque, or ashram, then go watch your favorite team. This one really helped me to humbly understand and allow the concept that there is equal value in my brother's watching games all weekend, as there was in my meditating all weekend in an ashram.

Appendix B
Soul Incarnation

Since I first learned about the soul and the idea of past lives, I pondered the question of how the population of incarnated human beings can continue to grow if, in fact, our souls are returning for lifetime after lifetime in this great theater of Earth. I've had plenty of experiences, both personally and through the work with my clients, to prove to myself that it is true that we do come back to enjoy the contrast of this physical experience as humans, in many varieties of human bodies and life circumstances. But the question was always where do the new people come from that allow the population to keep growing? And if they are brand new souls, then wouldn't they be perfectly clear, already masters of manifestation, without the old wounds and imprints that the rest of us have collected over lifetimes of unprocessed contrast? There would be millions of them by now all around us. And where were they before they incarnated here?

I may have the answers to those questions, and many more thanks to an inspiring question from one of my students. Just like in physical nature where cells split and form two identical cells, which are referred to as daughter cells, I think that the soul is capable of replicating itself into two or more identical souls (luminous bodies). These "daughter" souls are as whole and complete as the original soul, containing all of the same wounds and imprints, or patterns as the soul from which they split. These holographic daughter souls are then free to incarnate into separate physical bodies, which would be just as unaware of their twin soul as they are of their own soul (remember the "keeping a secret even from ourselves" notion).

This not only explains the ability for the incarnate population to grow, but could also explain why many groups of people share common experiences throughout their lives, and in some cases, almost identical experiences. And if you ever met the other incarnation of your soul, there may be an immediate familiarity and recognition of similar experiences, based on identical soul imprints; although the actual manifestations and mechanisms of the imprints could, and would likely be, different. In other words, you wouldn't have necessarily married and divorced the same person, or been in the same car accident, or earthquake. This also explains why multiple incarnated beings today may have shared a common past life; for example, it is possible that a hundred people alive today, could have been Cleopatra in one of their past lives, or like in my case that poor boat builder from China. And of course, the question that always arises is why is it that in past life regressions they were always somebody famous? Perhaps the souls that have famous incarnations split more than those of lesser fame, or people with those kind of past life experiences are more prone to be on the leading edge of their own paths of self-awareness and healing, and would therefore ever bother to explore their past lives, or perhaps it is just delusions of grandeur, more often than not – who knows, who cares?

This has interesting implications relative to myths of origin. The first original soul splits into two or more, which then incarnate and begin to gather experiences, and eventually unprocessed energies and unique patterns. As incarnated bodies of the original souls die and return to the Earth, the souls again might split into two or more, and thus the population grows, in both numbers and diversity of experiences. And as we embark on our healing journey today, many lifetimes away from the original incarnation, we begin to clear away the imprints and unprocessed energies, and reveal more and more of the unfettered original soul; and hence, our return to clarity, moment of now, powerful Creator, Siddhahood, Buddhahood, immortal, Messiah, Christ consciousness (God and I are one). The list goes on, depending on the myth, religion, philosophy, or spiritual tradition under which you are operating. You may have also heard someone referring to somebody else as an "old soul." They mean that this person seems to be wise and mature, usually beyond the years of their current incarnation. How I interpret such characteristics is that the person has probably done much healing work through their previous lifetimes, and has therefore come into this lifetime relatively clearer than is typical and thus closer to their/our true nature.

And not to leave anybody out, the atheists and ones whose myths indicate that we are just a physical organism that shows up for whatever time we have here and then just die into nothingness, all I can say is that you may be right, and I wish you the very best while you are here for this one and only physical life experience. And for those who believe we are here just once, and then go to Heaven or Hell for the rest of eternity, you may be right. And, if you look further into the original teachings that told you about Heaven and Hell, you will also find the teachings about multiple incarnations and how the notion of eternal life fits into this model very well, and that Heaven and Hell may just be descriptions of the possible experiences here on Earth.

Therefore, the population of incarnate beings can grow and shrink, with nothing really gained or lost other than the opportunity for more diverse experiences. A soul never dies, nor does it get stuck forever in some non-physical limbo, without a body to incarnate into. Rather, since it may be one of multiple daughter souls, the soul can just merge with other daughter souls, or back into the parent soul, or further back to the original soul. This also explains many of the mythologies and beliefs about remerging with the One, or the Void, and the possibility of an person incarnated today having multiple simultaneous past lives, as well as, individual incarnate bodies today having multiple souls in residence, so to speak.

This leads us to the notion that death, or the dulling of our soul, that stalks Westerners little by little until we see people who are more dead than alive, but haven't had the courtesy of disposing of their bodies, as my teacher Alberto would say. For many of those people, the notion of physical death doesn't even move them. They have stopped asking and receiving altogether, and are a kind of physical limbo, waiting to die, so to speak. Those who are fully engaged in the living process of "ask and it is given," will continue to thrive and to have a reason to be physically alive, even if the population is greatly reduced, as some prophecies indicate. This helps explain the Judeo-Christian stories of the "end-days," when the dead will be raised to live on the Earth once again, a Heaven on Earth. I take this not to mean that all the dead bodies in cemeteries, and so on, will be re-souled, but that the currently living bodies that have been claimed by death, will regain their life, and once again be active creators of their own experiences, through the process of "ask and it is given."

So, it is possible to visualize the coming into being, and receding, of whole colonies of souls, including the energy bodies of all aspects of Creation, from the tiniest parts of atoms to whole

245

galaxies, just as colonies of algae flourish, then die, then reappear in the oceans. This is the Hindu description of the inhaling and exhaling of the Universe in great cycles, called Yuga's and that the Mayan's call the Baktun. Creation reaches out in great flourishes of experimentation and evolutionary fractal branches, some with dead ends, some that may never stop reaching further, splitting and mutating in order to experience what works and what brings delight to itself. Human souls in human bodies, or in less physical forms, may just be one tiny temporary branch, or may be one solid never-ending branch of this fractal. Without being able to fully grasp where we fit into this mega-cycle, and why, the question comes back to the main greeting and philosophy of my Q'ero teachers, namely "Allyuwanchu", which is translated as "How does your village live within you?" and, "How do you grow corn with that?"

Appendix C
Anatomy of Prayer and Ritual Ceremony

I was recently asked to come up with an anatomy of prayer and ritual - a kind of scientific diagram that describes how all ritual and ceremony have an impact on our experiences in this existence. I was asked to show and anatomy that was universal, regardless of religions and all manner of spiritual and scientific belief systems and organizations. So to come up with such a diagram, I will start with the view that all of Creation is a random free-for-all of both physical and non-physical individual entities, or spirits, each participating in the creation process for the potentially joyful experience, which results from the contrast of pleasure and pain. These individual spirits are ultimately connected to one spirit or Source that Native Americans call Great Spirit, and that Western and Eastern religions call God, or scientists call the Unified Field. That pretty much covers everything we know of, and much of what we can speculate that exists, as well as the core reason for its existence...in a nutshell for now. From this assumption, we are ready to move on to the reason why we engage in prayer and ritual ceremonies, and how they work.

In addition to the constant asking and receiving that is happening from the signals that an individual entity or spirit of any form is sending out, how that individual relates to the rest of the entities and is able to get them on their side and in harmony with them, makes a difference in the amounts of pleasure and pain that particular individual will experience. This concept is the basis of all ritual and prayer that is directed to those spirits, including our rituals for gaining physical friends, allies, lovers, and partners. As a side, I believe that no spirit is entitled to guide you in the sense of telling you what to do or think, but to simply back you up in your own decisions if and when you ask them to; and, they may turn you down if they are more compellingly or resonantly called elsewhere. After all, the basis of life is the freedom to choose and to create our own experiences whether we are in physical or non-physical – purely spirit - form.

The anatomy of prayer rituals from a Quantum Physics point of view, is a process of getting your signal to be a match to your desired experience such that the signal finds resonant signals in the cosmic soup/matrix/implicit order, until enough come together to coalesce into an actual experience, in some form or manifestation detectable by the senses or the mind. This is why "when two or more are gathered" to send the same signal, it is exponentially more powerful in its ability to create an experience, because the physical laws of energy waves are such that two resonant signals (of the same, or harmonic frequency) double in amplitude/strength when they come together. And each additional resonant signal continues to exponentially strengthen the original signal. Each action in a prayer ritual is design to initiate, refine/purify, and boost the participant's signals, and to ally as many non-physical helpers as possible, to join in and produce the most powerful "asking" signal possible. The more powerful and pure the asking signal becomes, the more quickly the experience is delivered; and, to the extent that the person continues to produce a matching signal, or at least a neutral/non-canceling signal, the more likely is that the participant will receive the experience in whatever manifested form is possible.

The Shamanic healing rituals are another form of prayer with a particular anatomy. The energy signals that we send out can also be stored in our luminous bodies as imprints, or as deliberately organized architecture. To illustrate, I'll use the analogy of tattoos, which are imprints on our skin, designed to send a visual signal or message with some meaning, or desired effect, and experience for ourselves or for other observers. The tattoo may serve you for a time or period in life, or, you may decide at some point that you no longer want to send out that signal. In that case, you can go to a doctor with a special laser device, and have it removed. Some of the lasers are subtle, and leave no visual residue or scarring, and some may be too powerful, and leave evidence of the procedure through scarring or remnants of the previous pattern/tattoo. That is analogous to a healing that removes the Energetic imprints from your luminous body, such that they are no longer sending out a signal that is attracting unwanted experiences. And it is analogous to a healing that can happen in a subtle way versus a healing that can be too intense, which depends on the individual and their patterns. I came to a point in my own healing process, where some of the methods that I once found profoundly healing, began to become more traumatizing than healing: because they became simply too intense relative to the degree of sensitivity that my body, mind, and soul had reached. Another way to describe this would be that the healing process is similar to how a sculptor ends up with a statue of fine detail, like the David, from a rough block of stone. They will use big hammers and chisels in the beginning to clear away large chunks of stone, and by the end, they are using only fine brushes.

Similar to the storing the energy patterns from unhealed wounds, Shamanic rites of initiation, or rites of passage, are forms of prayer rituals that deliberately install and store energy patterns in our luminous body. Using the tattoo analogy once again, you can choose to get a tattoo that represents a very strong signal to the world about something you do want to experience and be identified with. For example, something that says, "Don't mess with me," or "I'm a healer," or "I'm a musician," or "I'm an artist," or "I'm a visionary," or "I'm a Maori warrior," and so on. This is analogous to receiving the Shamanic rites that install particular energy configurations into our luminous spirit body, or soul, and reorganize our luminous architecture. For example, from the Q'ero tradition, the rites of protection called the *Bands of Power* send the signal, "I am protected." The rites of clairvoyance, called the *Kawak Rites,* say to you and others, "I can see to the depths of everyone's soul." The totem rites called the *Ayni Karpay* say, "I have allies whose characteristics and instincts I can call on and embody anytime." The healer's rites called the *Pampamesayoq* say, "I am allied with the elements of nature." The teacher's rites called the *Altomesayoq* say, "I am allied with the energies and wisdom of the mountains and stars." The visionary rites called the *Kuraq Akuyek* say, "I am allied with the creators that dream the world into being." As these rites say what they are meant to say, so it becomes true for you because of those dominant signals being sent out from your luminous body. And you can see how this process can be carried into any walk of life. For example, a rite that imprints your luminous body with a signal that says, "I am a great writer, surfer, mother, producer, or all of the above, and so on" will help you be that. Each of those walks of life, have their own forms of rites of passage that have an effect on the core of our being, our Soul, that then works its way through the all of the layers and ultimately into our Literal experiences.

Therefore, there is no great meaning or purpose to life other than random pleasure and pain, and getting as much of one or the other as you prefer and are capable of creating, as well as being willing or not to ally with others in your quest for greater joy. And throughout known history, we can see that claiming any other purpose or meaning of life, or claiming to have the only view, explanation, and ceremonial approach that is true or that works, has ultimately led to self-righteousness, judgment, suffering, and war. Instead, if people are able to recognize and learn this basic anatomy of prayer and ritual, and then go out and use it in any way that works for them, and if we collectively allow for as many different ways as there are people, then we increase the possibility of greater allowing and harmony, and therefore greater grace, joy, and community from more free and empowered individuals. All the while, the rich diversity of Creation continues to grow and create new experiences for all participants.

An Invitation by the Author

If you have written notes about your vision, and/or wish to
elaborate on or clarify my vision, I invite you to share them with
me. I would appreciate hearing about your experiences from
reading this book. Also, there is nothing I love more than
addressing questions, and will make every effort to answer them
for you. My email address is jon@dreamingintobeing.com.

About the Author

Jon Rasmussen is a practitioner of the Shamanic arts for clients all over the world, and includes time for teaching, lecturing, writing, and project consulting. He was born in San Jose, California on November 23, 1963 at 6:09pm (for those who love astrological charting) the youngest of three boys. Jon's mother (a medical assistant) and father (an accountant) came from modest upbringings in Chicago, and Atlantic, Iowa. As a child and young adult, he was highly intuitive, sensitive, artistic, and intensely curious about life, science, and psychology. To the extent possible in a modern suburban setting, Jon began his own Shamanic training through intense study, experimentation, and near-death experiences. Taking all aspects of his life to the limit, he began a regiment of intense physical training involving gymnastics, bodybuilding, martial arts, yoga, and various other sports including training horses in dressage and polo. Jon obtained a Bachelor of Science Degree in Electrical Engineering and a Minor in Literature from the California Polytechnic University in San Luis Obispo California. He worked in the high tech industry of computer chip manufacturing and software for 12 years in various roles from engineering design and training to product management, including certification, licensure, and work within the financial services sector.

His work and personal interests have allowed him to travel and study all over the world. With the same intensity he applied to the hard sciences, Jon has studied and practiced many of the spiritual, metaphysical, healing, and religious traditions of the world, both ancient, and "new age." Jon's scientific background and healthy skepticism have helped him to maintain a high level of rapport and credibility with a wide range of people and their belief systems and worldviews. This has helped to make his work a true bridge between the worlds, and among this diverse human experience, thus having the broadest possible practical impact and personal fulfillment.

Jon has graduated from the Healing the Light Body School of the Four Winds Society, the Thetahealing and Teachers Training of Vianna Stibel's Nature's Path. Other certification and aspects of his education and practice in the healing traditions include various modalities of Massage, Reiki, Jin Shin Do, Tai Chi and Chi Kung, Feng Shui, Holotropic Breathwork, The Self-Realization Fellowship and Siddha Yoga courses and initiation, self-study of various schools of Modern Psychology, Neuro-Linguistic Programming, the teachings of Abraham-Hicks, The Flower of Life and Merkaba Meditation Training, Childhood Education, Organic Farming, Naturopathy, and informal training and initiation with various shamans from North and South America and Asia.

Jon always accepts opportunities to take his work and clients to places they have not been before, both internally and externally. Although uncomfortable and reluctant at times, Jon finds himself pushing the envelope of conventionality in all aspects of life, even Shamanism itself. A true visionary, he is always prepared, although seldom ready for the next step, and takes it anyway. Jon's most recent adventure has found him doing his shaman work, and bodywork, for the unique five-star resort hotel the Post Ranch Inn located in Big Sur, California. Before joining the Post Ranch Inn, Jon worked closely with a group of psychologists and psychiatrists in a highly successful collaborative effort. Jon continues to maintain a thriving private practice. He collaborates and integrates the Shamanic knowledge and practices into various walks of life, for example, recently working with a world-renowned architect to incorporate sacred geometry, energy tracking, and ceremony into his projects. For information on Jon's work and to schedule sessions or events with Jon, visit his website at www.dreamingintobeing.com. For information, reservations, and scheduling sessions at the Post Ranch Inn, visit www.postranchinn.com. For in-depth training and research in Shamanism, visit The Four Winds Society at www.thefourwinds.com.

In late 2007, Jon co-founded a company to create a feature film based on the life of Dr. Alberto Villoldo and a documentary film on modern Shamanism as well as other multi-media projects to help bring Shamanism and other consciousness raising bodies of work further into the mainstream of modern culture. For more information visit www.dreamshift.com.

Now
Bury this Book in the Earth
And Go Out and Have Fun
For
The Words Can Never Fully
Capture the Knowing Within
Your Eternal
And Playful Heart and Soul,
Always Connected to the
Source
And to the Wisdom, Beauty,
Well-being, and Wonder of
Nature.

Made in the USA